LEADING WITH EMOTIONAL INTELLIGENCE

*Unlocking The Power of Emotions
One Step at a Time*

Cedrick LaFleur / Tywauna Wilson

Copyright ©2024 by Cedrick LaFleur and Tywauna Wilson. United States.

All rights reserved.

No part of this book may be reproduced, stored in a retrieval system, or transmitted in any form or by any means, electronic, mechanical, photocopying, recording, or otherwise, except for the use of brief quotations to be used in a book review without prior written permission from the publisher.

Printed in the United States

Publisher: Trendy Elite Media Group

For Permissions requests or bulk orders: Write to "Attention: Permissions Coordinator" at info@trendyelitellc.com

Paperback ISBN: 979-8-9873658-6-1
Hardback ISBN: 979-8-32-752030-1

This book is intended to provide personal growth strategies that will assist readers in their journeys. This book is not intended to provide financial, health, or legal advice. Please seek appropriate counsel on financial, health, or legal matters.

DEDICATION

This book is dedicated to all leaders working with diverse teams. It takes courage and determination to lead a team, and we commend you for taking on this challenge. May the pages of this book guide you in cultivating your emotional intelligence so that you can lead with empathy, understanding, and resilience. Even if your journey into leadership is just beginning, we believe in your ability to have meaningful impact on those around you. Keep striving, growing, and leading with the heart.

EXECUTIVE SUMMARY

This book is your blueprint for leveling up as a leader through the power of emotional intelligence. The stage will be set by defining emotional intelligence and understanding its intricate ties to mental and physical well-being. Discovering practical strategies for navigating workplace emotions, gaining insights into managing diverse feelings, and understanding the crucial difference between optimism and pessimism. Additionally, you will learn how to create a personal vision statement and the vital skills of validating others' emotions. This journey will allow you to leverage emotional intelligence and make an impact as a leader, one intentional step at a time.

TABLE OF CONTENTS

Dedication iii

Executive Summary v

Introduction ix

Chapter 1: What Is Emotional Intelligence? 3

Chapter 2: Skills in Emotional Intelligence in the
          Digital Age 13

Chapter 3: Verbal Communication Skills 29

Chapter 4: Nonverbal Communication Skills 49

Chapter 5: Social Management and Responsibility 63

Chapter 6: Gaining Control of Our Emotions 77

Chapter 7: Enhancing Emotional Intelligence with
          Artificial Intelligence 93

Chapter 8: Navigating Online Relationships 103

Chapter 9: Emotional Intelligence in Business
          Practices 113

Table Of Contents

Chapter 10: The Global Impact of Emotional
                Intelligence in Business 121

Chapter 11: Unlocking the Power of Emotional
                Intelligence 131

Notes 137

Acknowledgments 139

About the Authors... 141

INTRODUCTION

Emotional intelligence, also called EQ, is the ability to be aware of and manage emotions and relationships. This is a pivotal factor for personal and professional success. IQ will get you in the door, but it is your EQ, your ability to connect with others, and manage the emotions of yourself and others, which will determine how successful you are in life.

We have all worked with, and listened to, brilliant people. Some of them were great, while others were not. The mean and meek, and all those in between, can teach us more than they realize. When we look at truly extraordinary people who inspire and make a difference, you will see that they do this by connecting with people at a personal and emotional level. What differentiated them was not their IQ, but their EQ – their emotional intelligence. This book will help you develop your emotional intelligence.

With this book, you will learn:

- Understand what emotional intelligence means
- Recognize how our emotional health and physical health are related
- Learn techniques to understand, use, and appreciate the role of emotional intelligence in the workplace
- Understand the different emotions and how to manage them
- Create a personal vision statement

Introduction

- Understand the difference between optimism and pessimism
- Validate emotions in others

> **The key to improving Emotional Intelligence is Practice, Practice, Practice**

STORY OF 2 HORSES: EMOTIONAL INTELLIGENCE
-Jagriti Vyas

Emotional intelligence exists in our personal lives, which includes our personal and professional lives from childhood until death.

Here is an excerpt of a short story that I recently read that once again drives the concept of Emotional Intelligence that is, or should be, at work in our life...

Just up the road is a field with two horses in it. From a distance, each horse looks like any other horse. But if you get a closer look, you will notice something quite interesting...

One of the horses is blind.

His owner chose not to put him down but made him a safe and comfortable barn to live in. If you stand nearby and listen, you will hear the sound of a bell. It comes from a smaller horse in the field. Attached to the horse's halter is a small copper-colored bell. It lets the blind friend know where the other horse is so that he can follow.

Introduction

As you stand and watch these two friends, you will see that the horse with the bell is always checking on the blind horse, and that the blind horse will listen for the bell and then slowly walk to where the other horse is, trusting he will not be led astray.

When the horse with the bell returns to the shelter of the barn each evening, he will occasionally stop to look back, making sure that the blind friend is not too far behind to hear the bell.

Think of your personal and professional life up to date: There are a lot of instances where you do the role of the blind horse and other times when you become the horse with the bell.

The blind horse signifies the times when we need to be inspired and motivated, so that we realize and are reminded of our infinite potential and strength. At other times, we become the horse with the bell – that is, the source of inspiration and motivation to guide others so that they can find their way through and achieve what they are capable of.

Therefore, it is said **"The secret of happiness is not in doing what one likes, but in liking what one does."**

Only about 36% of people in the world are emotionally intelligent.

PART I:
SETTING THE FOUNDATION FOR LEADERSHIP EXCELLENCE

CHAPTER 1
WHAT IS EMOTIONAL INTELLIGENCE?

> *Emotional intelligence accounts for nearly 90% of what sets high performers apart from peers with similar technical skills and knowledge.*

Emotional intelligence is the ability to recognize, understand, and manage one's own emotions, as well as recognize, understand, and influence the emotions of others. It involves bringing cognition to our emotional responses and being aware of the emotions that drive specific behaviors. Developing emotional intelligence is crucial in both personal and professional life, as it teaches us how to communicate professionally and empathetically.

Emotional intelligence plays a significant role in decision making and behavior. In the workplace, emotional intelligence strengthens teams by controlling and expressing emotions in a way that positively affects others. Emotionally intelligent team members recognize their own strengths and motivations and contribute them to the advancement of the team, leading to efficient decision making and increased productivity.

Setting goals is essential for success, and emotional intelligence helps create effective personal and team goals. By engaging us emotionally, emotional intelligence encourages commitment and motivation to see goals through. It also supports decision making by considering the choices that shape our future.

What Is Emotional Intelligence?

Emotionally intelligent team goals incorporate collaboration, empathy, and adaptation, creating a sense of purpose, and guiding each team member forward.

Emotional intelligence is also crucial in the hiring process. While hard skills are important, emotional and social intelligence are highly valuable skills for all workers. Verbal and nonverbal communication play a significant role in interviews, and emotionally intelligent candidates demonstrate their ability to manage their own emotions and influence the emotions of others. Effective feedback in the workplace is valuable, and emotional intelligence helps give and receive feedback to encourage improvements and make important decisions.

Emotional intelligence positively affects personal and professional relationships. Building rapport is crucial in managing relationships as it helps individuals feel understood and supported. This creates deeper connections and removes barriers to communication and trust. Responding instead of reacting is a powerful skill for emotionally intelligent people, allowing them to adjust their emotions to meet the surrounding environment and maintain healthy connections. Showing gratitude and finding common ground are also important in building relationships and creating a positive atmosphere.

Emotional intelligence is key to success in both personal and professional life. It allows us to navigate through social complexities, communicate effectively, make informed decisions, and build strong relationships. By developing emotional intelligence, we unlock the power of emotions and unleash our full potential.

Dan Goleman concluded in his book Emotional Intelligence at Work that when IQ and technical skills are similar, soft skills such as emotional intelligence, critical

What Is Emotional Intelligence?

thinking, assertiveness & self-confidence account for 90% of what makes people move up the ladder of success.

In other words, you need to develop your emotional intelligence.

Emotional Intelligence is a way of recognizing, understanding, and choosing how we think, feel, and act.

- It shapes our understanding of ourselves and our connections with others
- It defines how we grow and what we learn about ourselves and those around us
- It allows us to set the right priorities
- It determines the majority of our daily actions and interactions

It involves bringing cognition to our emotional responses and being aware of the emotions that drive specific behaviors. Developing emotional intelligence is crucial in both personal and professional life, as it teaches us how to communicate professionally and empathically.

The concept of emotional intelligence has been around since Aristotle. He wrote: "Anyone can become angry – that is easy. But to be angry with the right person, to the right degree, at the right time, for the right purpose, and in the right way – that is not easy."

Even back then, great philosophers understood the importance of managing your emotions.

Emotional intelligence plays a significant role in decision making and behavior. In the workplace, emotional intelligence strengthens teams by controlling and expressing emotions in a way that positively affects others. Emotionally intelligent team members recognize their own strengths and motivations and contribute them to the advancement of the team, leading to efficient decision making and increased productivity.

To help us understand these concepts, let us look at the thoughts of the experts.

Reuven Bar-On, Ph.D.

"Emotional intelligence is an array of personal, emotional, and social competencies and skills that influence one's ability to succeed in coping with environmental demands and pressures."

John Mayer, Ph.D. and Peter Salovey, Ph.D.

"[Emotional intelligence is] the ability to perceive, appraise, and express emotion accurately and adaptively; the ability to understand emotion and emotional knowledge; the ability to access and/or generate feelings when they facilitate thought (use); and the ability to regulate emotions in ways that assist thought (manage)."

Daniel Goleman

"Emotional intelligence is the capacity not only to be aware of and able to express our emotions, but also to manage and moderate them effectively. Emotional intelligence is what prevents anger from turning into rage and sadness into despair."

Setting goals is essential for success, and emotional intelligence helps create effective personal and team goals. By engaging us emotionally, emotional intelligence encourages commitment and motivation to see goals through. It also supports decision making by considering the choices that shape our future.

What Is Emotional Intelligence?

Emotionally intelligent team goals incorporate collaboration, empathy, and adaptation, creating a sense of purpose, and guiding each team member forward.

Emotional intelligence is also crucial in the hiring process. While hard skills are important, emotional and social intelligence are highly valuable skills for all workers. Verbal and nonverbal communication play a significant role in interviews, and emotionally intelligent candidates demonstrate their ability to manage their own emotions and influence the emotions of others. Effective feedback in the workplace is valuable, and emotional intelligence helps give and receive feedback to encourage improvements and make important decisions.

During the interview process, it is important for employers to understand the emotional intelligence levels of candidates. They can do this by asking high-gain emotionally intelligent questions versus the typical hard skill questions. High technical knowledge does not guarantee that the candidate has a high emotional intelligence. The following are some questions you should ask to gauge emotional intelligence:

1. How do you handle colleagues who challenge your ideas?
2. Can you give me an example of how your mood or attitude, either positive or negative, affects your work?
3. Do you think it is important to build rapport with colleagues, and how do you do it?
4. How do you feel when you are asked to do new tasks at work, and how do you approach those situations?
5. If you were to start a business, what would your core values be?
6. Can you give me an example of a time when your supervisor gave you negative feedback?

What Is Emotional Intelligence?

Conversely, employees can use the following questions to boost their emotional intelligence. This will help enhance your ability to influence, impact, and empower others. In addition, it will improve your ability to obtain the next promotion.

1. How do I react in moments of difficulty?
2. Why do I react in that way, and how can I improve?
3. Do my reactions help or harm me?
4. How did this situation fit into the big picture? That is, how will I feel about it in an hour? A week? A year?
5. What may I have misunderstood or be getting wrong, especially in the heat of the moment?
6. What would I change about my reaction if I could do it again?
7. How do I help motivate my colleagues/employees that I work with or supervise?
8. How do you deal with colleagues who are not doing their work or who perform work poorly?

Emotional intelligence positively affects personal and professional relationships. Building rapport is crucial in managing relationships as it helps individuals feel understood and supported. This creates deeper connections and removes barriers to communication and trust. Responding instead of reacting is a powerful skill for emotionally intelligent people, allowing them to adjust their emotions to meet the surrounding environment and maintain healthy connections. Showing gratitude and finding common ground are also important in building relationships and creating a positive atmosphere.

> A person who is in touch with his or her feelings will have a stronger chance of effectively leading those he or she is responsible for leading.

What Is Emotional Intelligence?

Benefits of Emotional Intelligence

Emotional intelligence recognizes feelings and responds in an appropriate and attentive manner. These skills and abilities heighten personal performance, empower relationships, and guide teamwork in a people-centric and results-oriented manner.

Some areas influenced by emotional intelligence include the following:

Communication	Productivity/Performance
Decision-Making	Relationship Satisfaction
Leadership	Customer Service
Sales	Conflict Management
Teamwork	Overall Effectiveness

At work, there are numerous benefits. There are both **increases and decreases** that **positively** impact performance when EQ is strong:

- Enhanced Employer/Employee Relations
- Improved Performance/Productivity
- Higher Attention to Task/Focus
- Greater Motivation and Satisfaction
- Improved Confidence and Self-Efficacy
- Better Problem Solving and Creativity
- Enhanced Leadership, Influence, and Team Performance
- Increased Collaboration and Synergy
- Improved Work Climate and Culture
- Better Interpersonal Connection and Effectiveness
- Greater Initiative and Commitment

- Reduced Stress
- Lower Levels of Bias and Mistrust
- Reduction in Absenteeism
- Significant Decrease in Turnover
- Decreased Burnout
- Minimized Negative Emotions
- Decreased Negative Interactions Due to Stress
- Fewer Aggression and Hostility Issues
- Less Safety-Related Violations
- Fewer On-the-Job Accidents
- Lower Worker's Compensation
- Fewer Disengaged Workers

Source: Assessment 24x7

The Six Seconds Model

Another way of thinking about emotional intelligence is the Six Seconds model, in which theory is turned into practice. To provide a practical and simple way to learn and practice emotional intelligence, Six Seconds developed a three-part model in 1997 as a process – an action plan for using emotional intelligence in daily life.

This model of EQ-in-Action begins with **three important pursuits:** to become more aware (noticing what you do), more intentional (doing what you mean), and more purposeful (doing it for a reason). This process is like a circle that never stops, it continues. As you use it, you will get better at it and improve your EIQ each time.

Ask yourself these three questions during the process.

1. What do you want?
2. How do you want to get there?
3. Why do you want it?

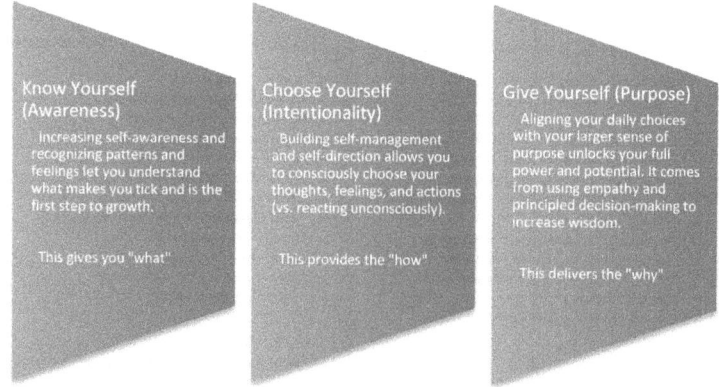

Source: 6seconds.org

Know Yourself gives you the "**what**" – when you Know Yourself, you know your strengths and challenges, you know what you are doing, what you want, and what to change.

Choose Yourself provides the "**how**" – it shows you how to take action, how to influence yourself and others, how to "operationalize" these concepts.

Give Yourself delivers the "**why**" – when you give yourself, you are clear and full of energy, so you stay focused on why to respond in a certain way, why to move in a new direction, and why others should come on board.

Emotional intelligence is key to success in both personal and professional life. It allows us to navigate through social complexities, communicate effectively, make informed decisions, and build strong relationships. By developing emotional intelligence, we unlock the power of emotions and unleash our full potential.

Examples of Emotional Intelligence in the Workplace

As personalities differ from person to person, the creation of emotional intelligence in the workplace requires effort. Anyone who has ever worked in a toxic work environment can attest to the importance of increasing empathy in this space.

Some examples of what emotional intelligence in the workplace are as follows.

- People express themselves openly and respectfully, without fear of offending coworkers.
- Resilience is evident when new initiatives are introduced.

What Is Emotional Intelligence?

- Flexibility is present.
- Employees spend time together outside of work.
- Freedom of creativity is celebrated and consistent.
- Active listening during meetings is the norm.
- Employees find a compassionate ear when needed, as we all have bad days.

CHAPTER 2

SKILLS IN EMOTIONAL INTELLIGENCE IN THE DIGITAL AGE

> *95% of surveyed HR managers and 99% of employees believe that emotional intelligence is a must-have skill for every staff member.*

In today's work environment, possessing emotional intelligence is essential for personal, professional, and business success. Emotional intelligence not only involves understanding and managing one's own emotions, but also encompasses how we engage and collaborate with others, especially in digital settings where traditional cues of face-to-face interaction are absent.

This chapter explores the foundational skills of emotional intelligence, focusing on their enhancement through the lens of digital communication. We delve into how these skills can be effectively applied to foster stronger connections and more meaningful relationships in an increasingly virtual world.

Digital Communication and Emotional Intelligence

Since the Covid pandemic that was declared in 2020, the rapid shift towards digital interaction has required us to rethink traditional emotional intelligence. In digital forums, whether emails, instant messaging, or video calls, empathy and understanding take on new forms. Digital empathy involves reading nuances in text, interpreting silence or brief responses, and effectively managing the digital image we project. An understanding of how to convey and interpret emotions accurately without the benefit of nonverbal cues is required.

Practical Tips for Digital Empathy

- **Read Carefully:** Always take time to read messages thoroughly before responding. This ensures that you fully grasp the emotional context of the message.

- **Reflects Emotions:** Use language that reflects your understanding of the sender's feelings. For example, phrases like "It sounds like you're feeling..." can demonstrate empathy and validate the sender's emotions.

- **Use Emoticons and Visuals:** When appropriate, emoticons and visuals can help convey tone and emotion, adding a layer of personal touch to digital communications.

Case Study: Brooke's Digital Leadership Transformation

Brooke initially believed that successful leadership was solely about numbers, strategy, and decision-making; however, upon leading a multigenerational team, she encountered challenges stemming from their diverse experiences and perspectives. Confused by her constant conflicts with colleagues, Brooke discovered a book on emotional intelligence. She realized that her leadership approach lacked empathy, social awareness, and adaptability. She focused on improving these skills, particularly in her electronic communication.

For instance, when a team member expressed concerns about tight project timelines, Brooke's original approach might have been to insist on adherence to deadlines without discussion. After embracing emotional intelligence, her responses were transformed. She replied, "Thank you for sharing your concerns with me. I understand the tight timelines can be stressful, and I appreciate you and the team's hard work. Let's discuss how we can adjust the deadlines or redistribute the workload to help ease the pressure. Would tomorrow at 10 AM work for a quick team call to explore some options?" This response shows Brooke's growth in digital empathy by acknowledging the team members' feelings and stress, while also demonstrating her willingness to take actionable steps to address the concerns.

As Brooke began to realize the impact of her newly adopted empathetic approach, she encountered another challenge that tested her understanding of digital emotional intelligence even further. Another example occurred when client feedback caused changes to a project scope. Previously, Brooke might have simply informed her team about the changes and the expected compliance. Instead, she crafted an email that read: "Team, I've received some feedback from our client that requires us to adjust our project scope. I realize that changes can be challenging, and I am here to support you through this transition. Please review the attached document, and let's schedule a call tomorrow to discuss any concerns or suggestions you might have. Your input is invaluable, and together, we'll make this transition as smooth as possible." This email not only communicates the necessary information, but also fosters a supportive environment, making her team feel valued and heard. Reflecting on this interaction, Brooke acknowledges the importance of flexibility and open dialogue, which she carries into her next challenge.

Building on this success, Brooke faced a situation that involved a missed deadline. Instead of just pointing out the missed deadline, she wrote, "I noticed we didn't hit the deadline for a segment of the project. I am sure you are juggling a lot, and I want to help you meet your goals. Could we discuss how we might better support your efforts? Let's touch base tomorrow to talk through any obstacles you're facing." This message helps maintain morale and encourages a more open dialogue about difficulties, which enhances team cohesion and problem solving.

By implementing regular emotional check-ins via video calls and encouraging her team to share their feelings, Brooke saw a significant improvement in team dynamics. Her commitment to display empathy even in digital spaces transformed her leadership style, fostering a more inclusive and supportive workplace.

Common Myths About Emotional Intelligence in Digital Communication

- **Myth #1:** Emotional intelligence is less important in digital communication.
    - **Reality:** This myth persists because digital interactions often feel less personal than face-to-face encounters, leading some to underestimate the importance of accurately conveying and interpreting emotions. Misunderstanding this aspect can lead to miscommunication and a lack of connection in remote teams, thereby impacting collaboration and productivity.
- **Myth #2:** Effective digital communication involves complex verbiage.
    - **Reality:** Individuals often equate complexity with intelligence or professionalism. However, in digital communication, where cues are limited, simplicity ensures that the message is understood

by all, thus reducing the risk of confusion, and enhancing clarity.

- **Myth #3:** More communication is better.
    - **Reality:** The misconception that quantity trump quality may stem from the digital age's emphasis on constant connectivity. However, excessive communication can lead to information overload, diluting the importance of messages, and leading to disengagement.

- **Myth #4:** Emoticons and gifs undermine professional communication.
    - **Reality:** Some view emoticons and gifs as unprofessional or too casual for business communications. However, when used appropriately, these tools can effectively convey tone and emotion, enrich the communication experience, and prevent misunderstandings in remote work environments.

- **Myth #5:** Emotional intelligence skills cannot be effectively conveyed through text-based communication.
    - **Reality:** This myth likely arises from the challenge of transmitting nuanced emotional cues through the text alone. However, the strategic use of language, tone, and timing can powerfully convey empathy and understanding, which is crucial for maintaining professional relationships in digital spaces.

Skills In Emotional Intelligence In The Digital Age

Good Versus Poor Digital Communication Practices

Aspect	Good Practice	Poor Practice
Email Etiquette	Concise and clear language, appropriate use of subject lines, timely responses.	Overly long emails, vague subject lines, delayed responses.
Tone	Using a positive, respectful tone, even in stressful situations.	Using a harsh or overly casual tone that may be misinterpreted.
Empathy	Expressing understanding and empathy through words, acknowledging the receiver's feelings.	Ignoring or dismissing the emotions expressed by others in communications.
Listening	Demonstrating active listening by asking follow-up questions and summarizing points.	Failing to acknowledge messages received, giving irrelevant responses.
Responsiveness	Replying within a reasonable time frame, even if only to acknowledge receipt and set a follow-up.	Ignoring messages or taking too long to reply without explanation.

Skills In Emotional Intelligence In The Digital Age

Clarity	Being clear and precise in communication; avoiding jargon and explaining when necessary.	Using complex language, being ambiguous, or leaving room for misinterpretation.
Feedback	Providing constructive feedback gently and privately.	Giving harsh feedback publicly or in a manner that may feel confrontational.
Professionalism	Maintaining professionalism in all forms of communication.	Using slang, emojis, or informal language inappropriately.
Multimedia Use	Using visuals, emojis, and other multimedia elements appropriately to enhance understanding.	Overusing multimedia elements which can clutter the message and distract from the main points.
Cultural Sensitivity	Being aware of and respectful towards cultural differences in communication styles.	Ignoring cultural nuances that affect communication preferences and interpretations.
Privacy and Security	Ensuring all communication is secure and maintaining confidentiality where required.	Being careless with sensitive information or violating privacy policies.

| Adaptability | Adapting communication style to fit the context, platform, and audience needs. | Using the same communication style across different platforms and contexts regardless of efficacy. |

Relationship Management and Effective Communication

Relationship management is an essential skill in emotional intelligence. By effectively communicating with others and managing relationships, we can create a sense of belonging, trust, and security. Just as a chef balances flavors and textures, leaders must navigate the complex emotional landscape in digital and virtual communication to build rapport.

Strategies for Effective Online Relationship Management

- **Consistent Communication:** Maintain regular and predictable online interactions to build reliability and trust.
- **Virtual Presence:** During video calls, ensure that your body language and facial expressions are engaging and attentive to foster a sense of presence and attentiveness.
- **Feedback Mechanisms:** Utilize digital tools that allow for anonymous feedback on communication styles, helping find areas for improvement in your digital interactions.

Self-Awareness and Self-Management

Self-awareness and self-management are the foundation of emotional intelligence. They become particularly significant in virtual environments, where stress and miscommunication are prevalent. Being aware of one's own emotions allows us to respond to situations with emotional maturity, adapt to change, and make better decisions.

Tips for better self-awareness and self-management

- Self-assessment tools, such as personality tests or emotional intelligence assessments, help gauge strengths and identify areas of improvement.
- Set aside reflection time for introspection and journaling to track emotional trends and triggers.
- Attending workshops on stress management, conflict resolution, and emotional regulation techniques.

Empathy and Social Awareness

Empathy and social awareness play a crucial role in emotional intelligence. Empathy allows us to understand and share the feelings of others, fosters strong interpersonal relationships, and enhances team performance. Social awareness involves recognizing and understanding others' emotions, which enables us to respond appropriately and build rapport. Cultivating empathy and social awareness involves making a positive impact on others, creating powerful first impressions, maintaining composure, inspiring leadership, and gaining self-confidence.

Digital Empathy Checklist for Virtual Meetings

Do:

- **Prepare and share an agenda in advance** to set clear expectations and to allow participants to prepare emotionally and logistically.

- **Use video, when possible,** to facilitate more personal connection and allow for visual cues.
- **Actively engage participants** by asking for their input and acknowledging their contributions to make them feel valued.
- **Be punctual** to show respect for everyone's time and to manage the meeting efficiently.
- **Use participants' names** and encourage personal expression to foster a sense of belonging and recognition.

Don't:

- **Multitask during the meeting** as it can lead to missed emotional cues and make others feel undervalued.
- **Overlook quiet participants**; instead, gently encourage them to share their thoughts, ensuring that all voices are heard.
- **Ignore technical issues** that might affect participants' ability to engage and address them promptly.
- **Rush through the meeting** without allowing time for questions or clarifications, which can lead to misunderstanding.
- **Use overly formal language** that might create distance; go for a professional yet approachable tone.

Case Study: A New Leader's Journey of Self-Discovery

"Developing emotional intelligence skills helps us better manage stress, communicate effectively, and build stronger relationships across all digital platforms."

As Stacie embarked on her journey towards self-discovery, she encountered numerous challenges that tested her communication skills and emotional intelligence in virtual settings. By applying specific practices from the digital empathy checklist and practical tips for digital communication, Stacie was able to transform her approach and enhance her leadership.

Scenario #1: Enhancing Virtual Meeting Engagement

Originally, Stacie struggled to engage her team in virtual meetings. She often found herself multitasking, which led to missing emotional cues and a sense of disconnection. After integrating tips from the digital empathy checklist, Stacie prepared and shared meeting agendas in advance, set clear expectations, and actively engaged participants by asking for their input and acknowledging their contributions. This not only made the meetings more productive but also helped team members feel valued and seen.

Example of Improvement:

- **Before:** Stacie often spoke over others trying to assert her presence.
- **After:** She learned the importance of taking turns and started using the participants' names, encouraging personal expressions, and ensuring that all voices were heard, especially the quieter members. This change fostered a stronger sense of belonging and team cohesion.

Scenario #2: Fostering Empathy Through Written Communications

Stacie noticed that her written communication often lacked the warmth and empathy needed to effectively connect with her team. She took the "Practical Tips" to heart by infusing her digital messages with more empathetic language and occasionally using emoticons to better convey tone. She also made a point to ask for clarification rather than making assumptions, which helped clear up misunderstandings before they could escalate.

Example of Improvement:

- **Before:** Messages were brief and transactional.
- **After:** Messages became more considerate and inclusive, reflecting an understanding of the team's feelings and perspectives. This approach helped reduce misunderstandings and build a more connected remote team.

Reflecting on Stacie's journey, think about the following questions to improve your own emotional intelligence in this digital age:

1. How can we ensure clarity and avoid assumptions in digital communication?
2. What strategies can be employed to respect and optimize virtual spaces during meetings?
3. Why is it crucial to provide written follow-ups, and how can they be crafted to enhance understanding?

Conclusion

Emotional intelligence in the digital age is more than just a beneficial skill; it is also a critical component of successful communication and leadership in virtual settings. From fostering better relationships to enhancing workplace productivity, the benefits of applying emotional intelligence in digital interactions are far-reaching.

Embrace the Challenge: Challenge yourself to apply the principles and practices discussed in this chapter. Start by assessing your current level of digital emotional intelligence. Identify areas where you excel and areas that need improvement.

Steps to Enhance Your Digital Emotional Intelligence:

1. **Reflect and Evaluate**
   - Conduct self-assessments using online tools and quizzes designed to measure emotional intelligence.
   - Reflect on past digital interactions and consider feedback from colleagues or friends regarding your communication style and effectiveness.

2. **Set Specific Goals**
   - Based on your assessment, set concrete goals for improvement. For example, if you find that you struggle with managing your emotions in stressful digital interactions, aim to develop strategies, such as taking a moment to breathe or compose your thoughts before responding.

3. **Practice Actively**
   - Implement tips from the "Digital Empathy Checklist" in your everyday digital communication.
   - Engaging in role-playing exercises with a trusted peer to practice responding to different scenarios will help reinforce digital empathy and adaptability.

4. **Seek Feedback**
   - After applying these new practices, ask for feedback regularly. This can be achieved through direct conversations or digital tools that allow anonymous feedback.
   - Use feedback to make continuous adjustments and improvements to your approach.

5. **Commit to Continuous Learning**
   - Emotional intelligence, particularly in digital contexts, is not a static skill, as it requires ongoing attention and adaptation. Keep abreast of new research and insights into digital communication and emotional intelligence.
   - Participate in workshops, webinars, and training sessions to further develop your skills and stay updated on the latest communication tools and strategies.

6. **Document Your Journey**
   - Keep a journal of your experiences and reflections as you work to enhance your digital emotional intelligence. This documentation can be a valuable tool for understanding your progress and identifying patterns or areas needing additional focus.

Call to Action: Encourage Others

Share your journey and insights with your team or peers. Encourage them to also assess and improve their digital emotional intelligence. By fostering an environment in which emotional intelligence is valued and developed, you contribute to a culture of empathy and understanding that enhances interactions for everyone involved.

By actively engaging with the strategies outlined in this chapter, you are taking important steps towards not only improving your digital interactions, but also enriching your personal and professional relationships. Remember, the journey to enhanced digital emotional intelligence is ongoing, and every step you take builds towards more meaningful and effective digital communication.

"Emotional intelligence is a skill that can be developed, like a muscle that needs training."

CHAPTER 3
VERBAL COMMUNICATION SKILLS

> *"In leadership positions, 85% of the competencies for success lie in the EI domain, rather than in technical or intellectual abilities."* - Daniel Goleman

In this chapter, we explore the importance of verbal communication skills in enhancing our emotional intelligence and building strong personal and professional relationships. Effective verbal communication involves active listening, asking questions, considering the audience, choosing our words carefully, and being authentic. In addition, assertive communication plays a crucial role in expressing our thoughts and opinions constructively, managing conflicts, and staying calm under pressure. Lastly, we discuss strategies for giving and receiving feedback effectively, which is essential for personal and professional growth.

EQ is based on an internal loop. It begins with **awareness** of emotions and temperament. It continues through **understanding** and moves towards **discipline** and **management**. After the initial personal cycle, it **connects** to the emotions of others. This reminds me of Thomas Edison's story:

Thomas Edison was practically deaf. When hearing aids were developed, Henry Ford rushed to buy the most expensive pair on the market for Edison. In fact, he could barely hear so when he was in a group of people; he would normally sit there or walk out and go into his lab to work because he could not hear what they were saying. After Ford purchased them, he went to Ft Myers to give them to Edison. He said, "I just purchased the greatest thing for you: these new hearing aids. Put them on to try them out."

Edison looked at Henry Ford and said, "Oh no, I don't want those. He said if I start wearing those, I will have to start listening to all these conversations and opinions and mess up my work. Oh no, I would rather keep it just like it is now."

Active Listening: The Gateway to Effective Communication

Active listening is a fundamental skill that allows us to engage with others and understand their perspectives. To improve our active listening skills, we must set aside distracting thoughts and remove any external distractions. It is important to show that we are fully present by nodding occasionally, smiling, and maintaining good posture. Encouraging the speaker to continue through small comments like "mmm" or "I see" demonstrates our attentiveness. Interrupting the speaker, even if we disagree, should be avoided. Instead, we can paraphrase their message to ensure understanding. Once the speaker has finished providing feedback, asking questions helps deepen the conversation and establish a connection.

How do you practice active listening? By being very intentional. I used to tell my team that, when we practice active listening, we help the customer give us all the information we need to sell to them. This requires the listener to be willing to not talk, eliminate distractions, and focus on every word that the communicator is transmitting. This is difficult for most people to do. It requires the listener to lock into the other person(s).

Do this by sitting straight up in your seat, ensuring your feet are firmly on the floor, slightly leaning towards the person, and nothing is running through your mind, but what that person is saying. Do not think of the questions at this point. This will allow you to eliminate the need to talk during the moment, so you do not distract the person's thoughts.

The Top 4 Active Listening Skills

1. Be attentive.
2. Ask high-gain questions.
3. Ask probing follow-up questions.
4. Paraphrase.

Active listening requires our complete attention. Leaders need to make sure they do not fall into the trap, like the two guys hunting.

A couple of guys were hunting. One of them fell to the ground and appeared not to be breathing. His eyes rolled back in his head. His friend pulled out his cell phone to call 911. He tells her, "My friend is dead. What should I do?"

The operator calmly replies, calm down, I can help you. Let's first make sure he is not breathing. First, there is silence, and then she hears a gunshot. He comes back to the phone and says, ok, now what?

As this story illustrates, we can hear what is being said without listening to what is being communicated. The hunter heard what the operator told him and technically did make sure his hunting companion was dead. If he had been listening, though, I don't think he would have shot his partner.

The message here is that when we hear without really listening, our leadership is bound to suffer, and so will our followers.

The VALUE Technique

Use the VALUE technique when someone is talking.

V	**Validate**
A	**Ask questions**
L	**Listen**, especially listen to the vocal (the tone) as well as the verbal (the words)
U	**Understand** the meaning that can be behind the words
E	**Empathize**

Validation does not mean solving a problem or offering a solution. When we validate, we acknowledge that we heard what the other person was saying. When someone is talking, listen without interrupting. Paraphrase, nod your head, or make appropriate listening responses to what they have said to show that you are listening. Allow for pauses and silence.

The SOLER Technique

Use the SOLER technique while you are listening:

S	**Sit** quietly with your arms and legs uncrossed. Crossed limbs can be interpreted as unwilling to listen, closed-minded.
O	Maintain an **open** posture.

L	**Lean** slightly forward in the direction of the speaker.
E	Maintain **eye contact**. Be sensitive though – some people are uncomfortable with extended eye contact.
R	Stay **relaxed**. Pay particular attention to your shoulders and neck.

Asking Great Questions: Igniting Engaging Conversations

Asking great questions is a powerful technique that enhances communication and facilitates sharing of insights and knowledge. By asking thoughtful and open-ended questions, we can encourage others to express themselves fully and create meaningful conversations. It is important to consider the audience when formulating questions, taking into account factors such as age, familiarity, and seniority. Tailoring our communication to suit the audience allows for better impact and understanding. By considering language, behavior, and tone, we can make adjustments that resonate with our listeners and foster effective communication.

John Maxwell writes in the book, Good Leaders Ask Great Questions, *"Leaders must ask questions to develop and grow. This holds true during your first leadership assignment as well as throughout your career.* **The more answers they receive, the better equipped they become to lead."**

Here are a series of questions that leaders should ask themselves, questions leaders should ask employees, and questions employees should ask the leader.

Questions Leaders Ask Themselves:

"When you're working in the middle of an organization with leaders above you, your success usually takes place on someone else's terms."

Socrates said, "The unexamined life is not worth leading." An amendment to his point of view might assert, "The unexamined leader is not worth following."

John Wooden, the UCLA Bruins' legendary former basketball coach, developed seven questions you can ask daily to check your progress as a leader. Give honest objective answers:

1. **"Am I investing in myself?"**
   No investment will ever be more important for your development. Your self-investment determines the return you receive from your work and life. Believe in yourself with full confidence.

2. **"Am I genuinely interested in others?"**
   Great leaders prioritize the people they lead over any leadership framework. The people they lead know their leader can say yes to such questions as "Can you help me?" "Do you care for me?" and "Can I trust you?"

3. **"Am I grounded as a leader?"**
   The Romans staged giant parades to honor their most successful generals, who rode in chariots while everyone cheered. A slave stood behind the general being honored, positioning a laurel wreath over his head to acknowledge the leader's recent victory. The slave also would whisper to the general, *"Hominem te memento."* Meaning, "remember, you are only a man." Leaders must never think they are better than those they lead.

4. **"Am I adding value to my team?"**
   Coach Wooden would ask himself, "How can I make my team better?" Search out your personal answer daily. To improve your team, encourage, and support your people.

5. **"Am I staying in my strength zone?"**
   To reach your full potential, concentrate on building on your strengths, not on improving your weaknesses.

6. **"Am I taking care of today?**
   Leaders must be visionaries who are prepared for the future, but they must also focus on the day at hand when everything takes place. Strive to make each day your best.

7. **"Am I investing my time with the right people?"**
   Pay attention to the people on your team, especially those with the potential to become leaders. Select your team members according to their traits and abilities, such as the capacity to grow personally and professionally, strong values, good character, and so on.

"If you begin a task with certainties, you will probably end in doubts. But if you are willing to begin with doubts, you will likely end in certainties."

Questions for Team Members

"We get fixated on our own point of view and spend our time trying to convince others of our opinions instead of trying to find out theirs."

The questions you ask your team members are crucial to their self-development. The right questions enable them to dream, improve their focus, educate themselves, concentrate, become more productive, and grow. Their answers give you information about them and their work, which you cannot find elsewhere.

Ask team members the following 11 questions:

1. **"What do you think?"** – Understand and leverage your team members' thoughts and experience. Asking them for their ideas breeds loyalty. It is a simple question used to gather information, confirm a leader's intuition, assess someone's judgment or leadership qualities, teach other people how the leader thinks, and reveal how they process decisions. Asking this question elevates everyone's ability to thrive and empowers the leaders to gather essential information that otherwise might not be offered.

2. **"How can I serve you?"** – Demonstrate your care for your team. Expressing concern draws people to you. When a leader asks employees this question, it immediately communicates that the leader values and respects the employees. A true leader is first a servant. Asking this question forces a leader to remain humble by serving other people. It also provides opportunities for greater collaboration. It is the leader's responsibility to make sure the team members have what they need to succeed and get their work done. Leaders who are not asking employees how best to serve them may just be holding them up.

3. **"What do I need to communicate?"** – Show your employees that you recognize you are not infallible; supply any missing information once you discover where

your team members might be confused. Successful communication comes from knowing the context more than the content. A leader asks this question to his team members to try and find out who the people are, what the situation is, what happened before, and how they can connect and help them. These three specific internal questions can help discover better answers to this larger question:
- Who should I be talking to?
- What is the most important thing?
- What is the call to action?

4. **"Did we exceed expectations?"** – Win others' approval by going above and beyond their stated wishes. By asking this question, a leader can learn if someone feels as if they do not deserve what they were promised, and they can also learn where improvements can be made for the future. One of the most important things a leader can do is make sure they and the organization are delivering on what they promised. Regularly asking this question ensures future success for both the leader and organization.

5. **"What did you learn?"** – Stop and think about your experiences. Urge your team members to evaluate what they have been through. This question helps everyone to better understand and connect with the people around them. It should be asked regularly in a team setting, because it keeps team members sharp and growing. It prompts the leader and their team to evaluate their experiences and make an assessment. Leaders understand that experience is not the best teacher—evaluated experience is.

Verbal Communication Skills

6. **"Did we add value?"** – Help other people realize their full worth and potential. Show them their value. A leader's goal should be to add value daily to those around them. This should not just be true in the workplace but in every area of life for a leader. Adding value to other people provides a firm foundation for achieving success in other areas. A leader asks this question of their team members to ensure that they stay focused on adding value to the organization, the other teams, and their clients or customers.

7. **"How do we maximize this experience?"** – Get the most out of every development you experience.

8. **"What do I need to know?"** – Mine the knowledge bases and perceptions of those around you. Trust what you hear. This question alerts leaders to the problems and current climate of the office. It allows team members to give the leader an overview of a situation, provide vital information, and prioritize what they think to be the most important pieces of information.

9. **"How do we make the most of this opportunity?"** – One open window can lead to another. The people who are directly involved have the best sense of what may follow. A leader must continually think about and ask others to think about ways to make their opportunities better. Asking this question helps determine the best ways to maximize opportunities. It sets up a leader and their team for greater influence, innovation, and profitability.

10. **"How are the numbers?"** – Never take metrics for granted. All organizations need the right numbers to gauge their progress. Sound numbers show how you

Verbal Communication Skills

are faring against your competition. Knowing the numbers allows the leader to keep a pulse on areas of success and areas for needed improvements. A leader should want to know the numbers, even if he or she won't like them. Even with a good vision and a good team, an organization will never be successful if it does not think about the numbers. This question addresses three things for the team:

- It keeps their heads in the game by keeping them accountable.
- It demonstrates that every person on the team in charge of performance management needs to keep their eye on performance indicators.
- It drives the team members to perform better together.

Numbers count. They tell a story. They let you know what the score is. They show trends. They reveal weaknesses. They provide tangible evidence of how well the leader and team are doing.

11. **"What am I missing?"** – What you do not know can hurt you. When a leader asks this question, it displays a willingness to learn from others. Two of the fastest ways to connect with another person are by asking questions and asking for help. Most people are willing to offer their perspective if asked, and they feel valued when they can offer their wisdom and experience. A leader must try to create an environment in which they can ask the people around them this question.

"A well-worded question...often penetrates to the heart of the matter and triggers new ideas and insights."

Questions Every Employee Will Ask of Their Leader:

1. Does my leader care for me?
2. Can my leader help me?
3. Can I trust my leader?

Your team members will consciously or unconsciously ask these questions of every leader. As the leader, it is your responsibility to provide the answers to these questions by your daily actions and interactions. The questions are going to be answered one way or another.

Choosing Our Words: The Power of Language

Words hold immense power in shaping our interactions and relationships. They are the building blocks of verbal communication, and play a crucial role in conveying our thoughts and emotions. Choosing the right words or using our words in a positive way can make a significant difference in how others perceive us and how conflicts escalate. It is essential to avoid language that inflames situations or makes others feel negative. Words like "can't" and "but" should be used sparingly, as they can create resistance or excuses. Instead, using "I" statements encourages open and honest expression of concerns. Being mindful of our words and responses conveys confidence and professionalism, fostering effective communication, and building trust.

As a young leader, I did not necessarily focus on the words I used. I used my words unfiltered and used terms like, "I'm just being real with you," and "that's just me." As I improved my leadership emotional intelligence, I realized that I needed to change the words I used. I started thinking more about the Platinum Rule, "Treat others the way they want to be treated." As leaders, we can hold on to our old way of talking to our team members, or we can learn how to effectively communicate and connect with them. We were told as kids, "Sticks and stones may break my bones, but words will never hurt me." I am here to tell you that words can hurt just as bad as physical harm. Connecting with your people increases your influence in every situation.

This reminds me of the story that a keynote speaker once said:

The Power of Words

The speaker had a cigarette prop and acted as if he would light it. Then, he said this, What? Y'all think smoking kills? Let me tell you something. Do you know that the amount of people dying from diabetes is three times as many people dying from smoking? Yet if I pulled a Snickers bar, nobody would say anything. Do you know that the leading cause of lung cancer is not cigarettes? It's your DNA. You could smoke for years, and nothing would ever happen to you. This whole world against smoking is to restrict the farming of tobacco.

I use these arguments, even though I just made them up with a group of my friends. And the results? Five of them believed what I said. Two of them started smoking. Words, when said and articulated in the right way, can change someone's mind. They can alter someone's belief. You have the power to bring someone from the slums of life and make a successful person out of them, or destroy someone's happiness using only your words.

Does this seem to be too good to be true? A simple choice of words can make a difference between someone accepting or denying your message. You can have a very beautiful thing to say, but say it in the wrong words and it's gone. When my son was 4 years old, I caught him writing on the carpet with a sharpie. I screamed hey are stupid, don't do that again. The very next day, I walked in, and he was writing on the carpet again, but this time, he was looking at me, sort of like in defiance.

This time, I kneeled down and said, son, you are a big boy now. Big Boys do not write on carpets. He never did it again. The first time, I attacked his ego. No one wants their ego hurt. The second time, I complimented his ego. Everyone wants their ego stroked.

Words Leaders Should Use More Often

1. I trust you
2. I value you
3. I want to help you
4. I appreciate your contribution

Eight Statements Every Child Needs to Hear

1. I love you
2. I'm proud of you
3. I'm sorry
4. I forgive you
5. I'm listening
6. You did great
7. You've got what it takes

Authenticity: The Key to Meaningful Connections

Authenticity and honesty are vital for establishing genuine connections and fostering trust in personal and professional relationships. Being authentic means sharing real information and eliminating assumptions. It involves being honest when we do not have the answers rather than pretending or providing inaccurate responses. Avoiding certain issues can lead to misunderstandings. By being honest and transparent, we can create an environment that encourages others to do the same. Authentic social connections are crucial for the long-term success of organizations and contribute to overall emotional intelligence.

Assertive Communication: Constructive Disagreements and Staying Calm

"Don't raise your voice, improve your argument."

Assertive communication plays a pivotal role in expressing our thoughts and opinions constructively, managing conflicts, and staying calm under pressure. Constructive disagreements allow for the expression of differing viewpoints in a positive and productive manner. Emotionally intelligent individuals recognize the value of constructive disagreements and express their opinions in a composed manner that builds stronger teams. It is essential to listen for understanding, ask questions to ensure clarity, provide evidence to support our explanations, establish common ground, and use "I" statements to express our thoughts without making it personal. Remembering our goals and visions, as well as the big picture, helps us effectively navigate disagreements.

Staying calm under pressure is crucial in high-pressure situations that arise in the workplace. Conflicts can lead to emotional outbursts and negative effects on our physical and mental well-being. By staying emotionally grounded, we can overcome the pressures of conflict and stress, thus limiting their negative impact. Reframing negative experiences, training our minds and bodies, and developing positive responses are effective ways to stay cool under pressure. With a positive mindset, we can thrive in challenging situations.

In order to stay calm during difficult conversations you must be able to identify and recognize your emotions. The following is a "EI Blueprint" that will help you improve your leadership effectiveness by practicing reflection questions, along with skills and concepts.

Identify Emotions
Reflective Questions

How do I recognize emotions?
Where do I hold emotions in my body?
How do I know for sure that what I believe is true?

Skills and Concepts

- **Be empathetic:** Pick up on emotional and social cues to react appropriately. Work to understand others, read body language, and use other nonverbal communication.
- **Self-honesty:** Accept your own qualities and faults, and recognize your own patterns of behavior that help and hinder situations. Recognize that emotions can get in the way of accurately accessing emotions in others.

Understand and Manage
Reflective Questions

- Will my response help or hinder the situation?
- Can you increase your awareness of your actions so that you see their effects?

- Am I hearing the unspoken messages?

Skills and Concepts

- **Reason and motivation:** Weigh your decisions and behavior by identifying and prioritizing what is important.
- **Manage feelings:** Use simple techniques, like a pause for reflection, to act – not react.
- **Choose to affirm the positive:** Accept that you have a choice, that you can make a difference, that you are an important part of the community.
- **Develop social behaviors:** Respond to people's needs, build conflict resolution skills, and accept feedback.
- **Interdependence:** Recognize your place in the larger community; your awareness and decision making takes into account the short- and long-term consequences of your actions as well as the context/culture.

Use and Communicate

Reflective Questions

- What is this emotion telling me?
- Do I know how to use emotional language to help understanding?
- Am I healing or hurting?
- What will my emotional reaction have on others?
- Will this emotion help me reach my goal?

Skills and Concepts

- **Apply consequential thinking:** Evaluate cause and effect and anticipate outcomes.

- **Empathy:** Use your compassionate awareness to guide your choices.
- People will remember the emotion of the situation long after they have forgotten the words and deeds.
- Express emotions appropriately.
- **Practice integrity:** Hold yourself to high standards and do what is right, even when it seems hopeless.

Giving and Receiving Feedback: The Path to Growth

Effective feedback is invaluable in personal and professional growth. When giving feedback, it is important to tailor it to the individual, considering their strengths, weaknesses, communication style, and motivations. Feedback should be given face-to-face, with attention to tone and body language. A supportive attitude and solution-oriented approach enhances the impact of feedback. When receiving feedback, it is crucial to choose acceptance and assume positive intent. Being humble and curious, asking questions for clarification, and taking action based on feedback contribute to personal and professional growth.

Developing strong verbal communication skills is essential for enhancing emotional intelligence and building strong personal and professional relationships. Active listening, asking great questions, choosing our words carefully, being authentic, practicing assertive communication, staying calm under pressure, and giving and receiving feedback effectively are key strategies in mastering verbal communication. By honing these skills, we can unlock the power of emotions and create meaningful connections that foster growth and success.

The feedback loop is not only critical for the leader but is even more important for employees. As an employee, I looked forward to feedback. I always wanted to know what I could improve. I remember a specific field travel with my VP of Sales. He traveled with me to a call with the Laboratory Administrator at MD Anderson Cancer Center. After the call, I sent him an email to inquire about what I could improve on. He responded back that I did an outstanding job and just doing what I was doing. I responded by thanking him for the feedback, but I wanted to also know specifically what I could do better. I asked that because I knew in that call, I did not feel like I was being myself. I asked questions from our sales rubric versus asking the question in my authentic voice. Response really did help me going forward. He said, "Cedrick, don't worry about the sales rubric, the reason you have been successful was because you were always being authentically yourself, so keep doing that." He further said, the sales rubric is to help those that do not know what to do; it gives them a framework to follow. That helped me tremendously going forward.

So, for leaders, you need to always remember to be authentically yourself. As you continue to grow and develop, it will help shape the type of questions you ask, improve your active listening skills, and ensure you learn how to control your emotions. For employees, these tools will help you grow into high emotional intelligent employees.

CHAPTER 4
NONVERBAL COMMUNICATION SKILLS

> *The total impact of a message is about 7% verbal (words only), 38% vocal (including tone of voice, inflection), and 55% nonverbal." [percentages are specific to situations where emotional attitudes are being communicated]. –*
> *Albert Mehrabian*

Effective leaders need a variety of skills to connect with their teams and drive success. One such skill is the mastery of nonverbal communication, a critical tool for enhancing emotional intelligence and leadership presence. While words are important, our body language and facial expressions also play a significant role in conveying messages. These nonverbal cues can reveal a wealth of information about our emotions, intentions, and true reactions, allowing us to communicate more effectively and build stronger connections with others. Leaders must be mindful of their body language, facial expressions, eye contact, tone of voice, and gestures when communicating with their team. Nonverbal communication skills can be deliberately improved and practiced, setting the tone for the actionable insights provided in this chapter.

Body Language: Open to Success

Body language serves as a powerful tool in nonverbal communication, particularly among leaders who strive to connect with their teams. It encompasses two primary categories: open and closed body language. Open body language includes gestures such as uncrossed arms, an upright head, and a forward-leaning posture, which collectively broadcasts openness, warmth, and readiness to engage. Such postures are perceived positively and are crucial in establishing trust and persuasiveness. Conversely, closed body language is characterized by crossed arms, a rounded upper body or averted eyes, signal withdrawal, defensiveness, or lack of interest.

Consider a typical team meeting scenario: a leader practicing open body language by maintaining an upright stance and making direct eye contact can make team members feel acknowledged and at ease, encouraging them to participate actively in the discussion. In contrast, a leader who adopts a closed posture, such as sitting hunched over with arms crossed, may inadvertently convey disinterest or impatience, which could stifle open communication and diminish team morale.

Leaders must continuously be mindful of their body language to ensure it aligns with the positive messages they intend to convey, thereby enhancing their effectiveness and influence within the team.

Facial Expressions

Our facial expressions speak volumes, conveying a rich array of emotions without a single word. Often unconscious, they are a reliable indicator of our true feelings. Understanding the meaning behind different facial expressions gives us invaluable insights into how others are truly feeling. However, we must also be mindful of our own facial expressions, particularly in professional settings, because they can greatly influence how we are perceived by others. By focusing on subtleties such as the eyes, mouth, eyebrows, and nose, we can interpret the deep-seated emotions behind different expressions.

Imagine that you are leading a team meeting and presenting a new strategy. Your team members are somewhat unsure about this approach, but you feel confident and optimistic. Without realizing it, you might furrow your brow or press your lips tightly together, causing your team to perceive your confidence as doubt. By being aware of your own facial expressions and making a conscious effort to align them with your message, you can foster greater trust and understanding with your team. In doing so, you will create an environment in which your team feels empowered to express their thoughts openly and receive your message positively.

Eye Contact

Eye contact plays a pivotal role in nonverbal communication. Our eyes have the ability to convey a wealth of information and establish a personal connection between the speaker and the listener. Consistent eye contact throughout a conversation demonstrates interest and engagement, encouraging the speaker to continue sharing their message. Effective eye contact communicates confidence and honesty. Conversely, avoiding, or breaking eye contact can signal low self-confidence, guilt, or disinterest. It is crucial to be mindful of the cultural differences in interpreting eye contact, as various cultures may perceive its meaning differently.

Imagine yourself in a planning meeting. As you present your ideas, you maintain steady eye contact with your colleagues, signaling your confidence and genuine interest. This not only encourages your colleagues to actively engage with your presentation, but also fosters trust and openness among the team. Conversely, if you were to continually avoid eye contact, your colleagues may perceive this as a lack of confidence or disinterest. Therefore, understanding and utilizing the power of eye contact can significantly impact your effectiveness as a communicator and leader, ultimately enhancing collaboration and productivity in the workplace.

Tone of voice

In nonverbal communication, tone of voice and gestures are pivotal elements. Indeed, the way a message is delivered, including its pitch, pace, and timing, often surpasses the words themselves. Our tone has the power to convey an array of emotions ranging from aggression and confidence to anger or sarcasm. As such, being acutely aware of the subtleties of our speech and using appropriate gestures can add nuance and depth to our communication, thereby reinforcing the intended message. For example, a steady tone can reassure teams during a crisis. A manager might use a calm, lower-pitched tone to convey seriousness and control when announcing a setback or a challenging update, helping to stabilize team emotions and encourage focused problem-solving. A cheerful upbeat tone can boost morale during routine check-ins or when introducing new projects.

In a presentation to the sales team, the manager's tone projected enthusiasm, echoing her confidence in the new product. She spoke passionately and with a lively pace using gestures to underline key points and connect with her audience. In doing so, she vividly conveyed the importance of the product launch, engaging her team's attention and inspiring them to embrace the new strategy. Through her compelling use of tone and gestures, the manager not only communicated her excitement, but also instilled a sense of urgency and motivation within the team, setting the stage for a successful product launch.

Nonverbal Communication Skills

> "It's how you looked when you said it, not what you actually said."

Common Misconceptions of Nonverbal Communication

In the realm of communication, nonverbal cues often carry immense weight, serving as a silent yet powerful means of expression. While their significance cannot be overstated, misconceptions surrounding nonverbal communication abound, fueling misunderstandings and misinterpretations in various contexts. It is imperative to debunk these prevalent myths and grasp the nuanced intricacies of nonverbal cues, understanding their varied interpretations across cultures and personal differences. The holistic understanding of nonverbal communication necessitates vigilance against overemphasizing singular cues, overlooking contextual influence, equating tone of voice with intent, and believing in absolute meanings.

1. **Assuming Universal Interpretation:** One common misconception is that nonverbal cues such as body language, facial expressions, and tone of voice have the same meaning across all cultures and contexts. In reality, the interpretation of these cues can vary significantly depending on cultural norms and individual differences. For example, a thumbs-up gesture with a multinational team can be interpreted differently across cultures, leading to confusion and the need for clarification.

2. **Overemphasizing Single Cues:** Focusing too much on a single nonverbal cue, such as eye contact, and assuming it always conveys the same message. A leader could misinterpret a team member's lack of eye contact as disinterest, while the team member might simply be shy or may come from a cultural

background where direct eye contact is less common. Effective communication involves considering a combination of cues to accurately interpret meaning.

3. Ignoring Context: Some learners may overlook the importance of context when interpreting nonverbal cues. They might assume that a specific body language gesture always means the same thing without considering the situational factors influencing its interpretation. A manager could interpret crossed arms as a sign of resistance or negativity, not recognizing that the employee might simply be cold or more comfortable in that position.

4. Equating Tone of Voice with Intent: Another misconception is equating tone of voice solely with the speaker's intent. Although tone can offer valuable insights into emotions and attitudes, it is essential to consider other nonverbal cues and verbal content to grasp the full message.

5. Believing in Absolute Meanings: Falling into the trap of believing that nonverbal cues have absolute meanings that are universally understood, leading to misinterpretations and misunderstandings in communication. It is crucial to recognize the nuanced nature of nonverbal communication.

By dispelling these common myths, we open ourselves up to a deeper understanding of the nuances embedded in nonverbal cues, fostering stronger connections and clearer messages. It is essential to consider the multifaceted nature of nonverbal communication, questioning our assumptions and interpretations.

- *How might our cultural background influence our understanding of nonverbal cues?*

- *What nonverbal cues might we be neglecting or misinterpreting in our everyday interactions?*
- *How can we improve our awareness of nonverbal communication to become more empathetic and effective communicators?*

These questions prompt us to be more mindful and introspective, guiding us towards more meaningful and impactful communication.

Mastering Nonverbal Communication

Mastering nonverbal communication has the potential to elevate your emotional intelligence and significantly enhance your leadership abilities. Developing an acute awareness of your own nonverbal signals is a crucial first step in understanding the impression you make on others and effectively managing your influence. Adapting your nonverbal communication to different situations ensures that you can effortlessly navigate diverse contexts and cultivate stronger relationships across various cultures. Enhanced nonverbal communication skills contribute to increased emotional intelligence and effective leadership in several impactful ways:

- Better understanding of others
- Cultural awareness and adaptability
- Persuasive communication
- Enhanced relationship building
- Effective management and understanding of their emotions and of others

Practical Techniques to Enhance Nonverbal Communication for Leaders

Mastering nonverbal communication is not just about enhancing personal skills; it is also about transforming how leaders interact with and influence their teams. The following practical techniques are designed to build on the foundational nonverbal skills discussed in this chapter, aiming to turn theoretical knowledge into everyday leadership practices. By refining these skills, leaders can ensure their nonverbal cues consistently support their words, thereby deepening trust and enhancing team synergy

1. **Self-Reflection:** Engage in regular self-reflection exercises to analyze your nonverbal cues, focusing on body language, facial expressions, and tone of voice. Consider how your nonverbal signals impact the emotional atmosphere and leadership presence.

2. **Cultural Sensitivity Training:** Seek out training programs or workshops that focus on cross-cultural nonverbal communication, allowing you to adapt your nonverbal cues to different cultural contexts. This practice helps to build stronger relationships across diverse cultural backgrounds.

3. **Feedback and Mentoring:** Actively seek feedback from trusted colleagues or mentors to gain insight into how your nonverbal communication is perceived. Use this feedback to identify areas for improvement and refine your nonverbal cues accordingly.

4. **Professional Development:** Enroll in nonverbal communication training and development programs that cater specifically to leadership. This helps in honing your nonverbal

communication skills, leading to an increase in emotional intelligence and leadership influence.

Incorporating these practical techniques not only elevates a leader's nonverbal communication skills, but also contributes to a more emotionally intelligent and influential leadership style. By engaging in these strategies, leaders can effectively inspire action, foster inclusivity, and build strong, trusting relationships with their teams, thereby promoting a positive and empowering organizational culture.

Practical Application

At a prominent software development company, Elena, the project manager, observed that despite the technical expertise of her team, communication barriers and fluctuating morale often hindered project success. Recognizing that these issues often intensified under pressure, Elena decided to use the power of nonverbal communication to strengthen team cohesion and enhance operational efficiency.

Strategic Application of Nonverbal Skills

Elena noted her tendency to rush through meetings with a somewhat closed posture, which could inadvertently signal disengagement. To address this, she implemented key changes in her nonverbal communication style:

1. **Adopting an Open Posture:** During team gatherings, Elena consciously adopted an open posture—sitting upright and leaning forward slightly. This posture shift not only demonstrated her active engagement, but also invited openness from team members, marking a significant departure from her previously more reserved stance.

2. **Maintaining Eye Contact:** Elena committed to maintaining consistent eye contact with team members while they spoke, moving away from her habit of looking at notes or screens. This subtle yet impactful change underscored her attentiveness and respect for their input.

3. **Regulating Facial Expressions:** Understanding the influence of facial expressions, Elena focused on moderating her expressions to convey calmness and assurance, particularly during discussions of project challenges or critical feedback.

Practical Outcomes:

These intentional adjustments in nonverbal cues yielded the following benefits:

- **Enhanced Team Participation:** The shift to an open posture and direct eye contact nurtured a more welcoming and inclusive meeting environment. Team members responded by participating more actively, as evidenced by the uptick in questions and innovative suggestions.

- **Reduction in Misunderstandings:** Elena's focused efforts to align her facial expressions and body language with her verbal messages significantly decreased misunderstandings. Team members better understood her intentions, fostering clearer and more effective communication.

- **Boost in Morale and Productivity:** These improvements in nonverbal communication contributed to a more positive and supportive team atmosphere. The elevated morale correlated directly with enhanced productivity and fewer project delays, underscoring the effectiveness of thoughtful nonverbal communication.

Discussion Questions:

1. Reflect on a recent meeting where you felt misunderstood. How could better awareness of nonverbal cues have changed the outcome?

2. How can honing nonverbal communication skills contribute to amplifying emotional intelligence and inspiring innovative leadership practices within an organization?

PART II:
NAVIGATING THE LEADERSHIP JOURNEY WITH EMOTIONAL INTELLIGENCE

CHAPTER 5
SOCIAL MANAGEMENT AND RESPONSIBILITY

> *Organizations that value and widely use emotional intelligence are 3.2x more effective at leadership development.*

EQ is based on two competencies, measured in Recognition (Responsibility) and Management:

- *The ability to recognize, understand, and manage emotions (self or intrapersonal)*
- *The ability to recognize, empathize, and relate to the emotions of others (social or interpersonal)*

Research indicates that emotional intelligence can be learned and improved, seen as measurable differences that are directly associated with professional and personal success. Furthermore, it may be responsible for up to 80% of the success that we experience in life.

Social management is an essential element of emotional intelligence because it empowers us to navigate and nurture our relationships with finesse. By understanding and managing our own emotions, we can effectively communicate, resolve conflicts, and build meaningful connections. Let us embrace the power of social management and cultivate stronger bonds with the people around us.

Social management includes interpersonal skills and focuses on intelligence in generating results. This social intelligence fosters collaboration and connection to tap the power of synergy. Synergy is an interaction or cooperation giving rise to a whole that is greater than the simple sum of its parts. In other words, the team is more important than one individual.

There are four areas of Emotional Intelligence:

- Self-Recognition (Awareness)
- Social Recognition (Awareness)
- Self-Regulation (Management)
- Social Regulation (Management)

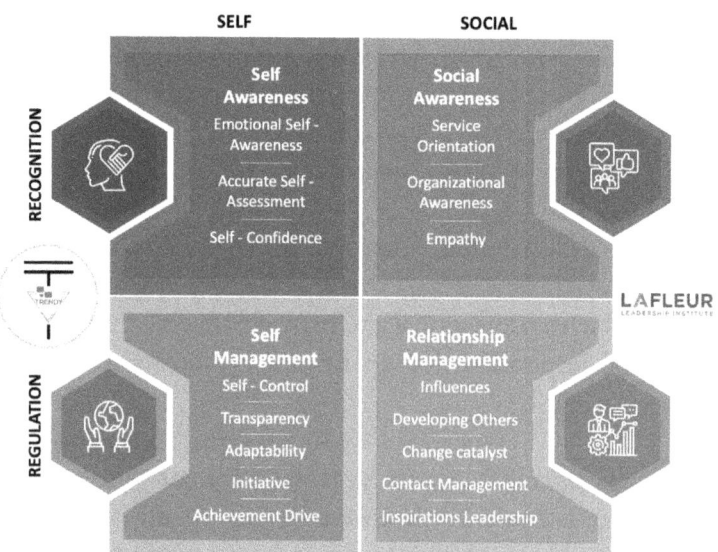

Social Management And Responsibility

In the fast-paced business world, social connections and effective communication are key to success. The ability to build and maintain relationships is a valuable asset that contributes to a happier and healthier workplace. By reflecting on our personal networks and the quality of our relationships, we can work towards improving and strengthening these connections.

Building rapport is essential in managing relationships. It involves creating emotional connections and fostering deeper relationships with others. Rapport helps individuals to feel understood and supported, creating a sense of belonging and trust. In a business setting, building rapport is crucial for networking, interviewing, and career advancement.

To build rapport:

- Look for opportunities to connect.
- Ask genuine questions.
- Remember names and details.
- Be genuine and friendly.
- Compare goals.
- Be respectful of others' time.

A powerful skill that emotionally intelligent people possess is the ability to respond rather than react in challenging situations. Reacting with emotional outbursts can lead to bigger problems and damage relationships. Instead, it is important to remain calm, take time to think through the situation, and process emotions in a healthy manner. This allows for better control and ownership of the problem, leading to healthier connections and resolutions.

Understanding cultural differences and biases is one of the most important skills that must be developed in a global ecosystem.

Social Management And Responsibility

In an increasingly interconnected world, individuals in social management often interact with people from diverse cultures and backgrounds. Adapting to cultural differences involves being aware of and respecting cultural norms, values, and sensitivities. This allows for more effective communication, reduces misunderstanding, and promotes inclusivity and diversity.

How do Inclusive Leaders become more aware of their own biases and assumptions regarding cultural differences?

Not surprisingly, our brains' automatic use of categories is particularly risky with respect to race. The widespread stereotype of black criminality makes it more likely that a cell phone will appear to be a gun if the man holding it is black rather than white (Correll 2007). Implicit bias refers to the process of associating stereotypes or attitudes towards categories of people without conscious awareness. Everyone has some sort of implicit bias.

- They have to ask themselves where are they biased. And answer it honestly.
- We all have biases. Every person on the planet has biases.

EXAMPLE:

- When you see someone with an earring in their nose or tattoos all over their body, you immediately come up with an idea in your mind about that person.
- What about when you see a motorcycle rider with a leather jacket and pants on, you come up with thoughts about that person.
- Here is a personal example from Cedrick: I went to a coworker's house once. I rang the doorbell; his wife answered the door. She immediately ran back and told him, "There is a black guy at the door." He came to the

door and yelled out, "Leslie that's Cedrick." She then came to the door, hugged me, and said, hello. I had spoken to her on the phone many times, but she had never met me in person. She knew that I was black, but she panicked when I rang her doorbell. This is an example of bias, assumptions, and stereotyping.

Reducing Bias

- If we want to reduce our implicit bias, we have to literally practice. What this means is that we need to take active steps to see people as they are, not to generalize based upon stereotypes.

What is the best advice you could give to a leader who wants to intentionally build an inclusive environment?

- If you want to intentionally be inclusive and learn about people of different backgrounds, then you just have to do it.
- If you want to know about a different culture: Go down the street to their church, restaurant, or a "event."
- If you want to know more about the LGBTQI community, go to an event and talk to them.
- If you want to know what it feels like to be in the minority, then go to an event or place where you will be in the minority, then you will get to feel firsthand.
- You will be surprised by the similarities you have.

Example: Join a group or choose an activity that includes people from other racial and ethnic groups. If you engage in these practices over a period of weeks, research shows that you will have lower implicit bias. Ideally, you will be part of a broader community of people.

Flexibility in Problem-Solving increases your ability to work effectively with others. Social management often involves addressing complex issues and finding solutions that meet the needs of multiple individuals and groups. Being adaptable allows individuals to think creatively, consider different perspectives, and explore alternative approaches. This flexibility in problem-solving enhances the ability to find mutually beneficial solutions and resolve conflicts effectively.

Showing gratitude is another important aspect of social management. By expressing appreciation for others, we can strengthen relationships and create a positive and supportive environment. Gratitude fosters a sense of belonging and encourages others to reciprocate, leading to stronger connections and happier workplaces.

Setting boundaries is a crucial life skill that contributes to social management. Emotional boundaries protect our values, time, and energy, and help us maintain control in personal and professional relationships. By establishing healthy boundaries, we can eliminate negative situations and create more positive and productive environments. The more you exercise your right to set a boundary, the more you will grow in emotional intelligence, too!

Strategies for setting healthy boundaries with others include:

- Recognizing discomfort
- Learning to say no
    - I am afraid I can't right now.
    - Unfortunately, I have something else going on right now.

Social Management And Responsibility

- o   I am honored that you asked me, but I simply can't right now.
- o   I wish I was able to.
- Being assertive but not aggressive
- Recognizing personal tolerance levels
- Speaking up for oneself

Embracing change and uncertainty are critical social management skills. Social management can involve navigating change and uncertainty, organizational changes, shifting group dynamics, or unexpected challenges. Being adaptable helps individuals to embrace change, remain resilient, and navigate uncertainty with a positive mindset. This allows more effective leadership and management in dynamic social environments.

Conflict resolution and negotiation skills are essential in social management. Conflict is inevitable in the workplace and the ability to handle emotional stressors is crucial. Acknowledging and managing emotions is the first step towards overcoming workplace obstacles. Disagreeing constructively is important for fostering innovation and progress within a team. Emotionally intelligent individuals understand the value of constructive disagreements and express differences of opinion in a positive and productive manner.

When resolving conflict, it is important to:

- Listen for understanding
- Ask questions
- Provide evidence
- Establish common ground
- Use "I" statements
- Remember goals
- Avoid making disagreements personal

For the moment, set aside your list of options. It's time to create a framework to evaluate those options. Try not to think about the different options as you create the criteria. Instead, focus on the wants and needs of both parties.

Criteria should explore what you want and do not want from the solution. You can also prioritize your criteria based on what is necessary to have and what you would like to have (also known as needs and wants). Identify any items on the list with which you would be willing to compromise. Remember that as the leader, it is your responsibility to lead this conversation with your employee or team. Do not go into the meeting without having completed your list of these things. If you do, emotions will come out and that will not lead to effective outcomes.

When you have thought through the criteria, wants, needs, and compromise areas, you will find it easier to stay focused and control your emotions. This is what a high EQ is all about.

Criteria	Want?	Need?	Shared with the Opponent?	Compromise On?

Being open to different perspectives is the key to conflict resolution and social management. Recognizing that our own viewpoint is not the only one that allows for open-mindedness and empathy. Emotional intelligence involves considering the perspective of others and understanding their motivations. By allowing others to express their arguments or beliefs, we can find ways to provide support and collaborate towards a shared goal. Shifting our perspectives can turn confrontations into learning experiences and promote effective collaboration. This is where you can gauge improvements in your EQ.

Ethical decision-making and social responsibility are closely linked to emotional intelligence. Emotional intelligence allows us to make ethical choices that consider the impact on individuals and society. Empathy and ethical decision-making go hand-in-hand; leaders with high emotional intelligence are more attuned to the needs and concerns of others.

Leaders with high emotional intelligence consider how their decisions today will impact future generations. They are more likely to prioritize long-term investments that not only generate profits but also promote ethical principles such as employee engagement and social responsibility.

How to tell if you need to improve your ethical decision-making and responsibility.

Rate yourself on a scale of 1-5: (Be honest with yourself)

- **1 = Need immediate improvement**
- **2= Need some improvement**
- **4 = I'm doing good, but working**
- **5 = I'm really developed**

1. Demonstrating curiosity and open-mindedness
2. Learning how to make a reasoned judgment after analyzing information, data, and facts
3. Making ethical decisions based upon mutual respect and appropriate culturally relevant social norms
4. Recognizing one's responsibility to behave ethically

Social Management And Responsibility

5. Anticipating and evaluating the consequences of one's actions
6. Recognizing how critical thinking skills are used both inside and outside of work
7. Reflecting on one's role to promote personal, family, and community well-being
8. Evaluating personal, interpersonal, community, and institutional impacts

If you rated yourself with more 4-5s, then you are moving in the right direction. If you rated yourself more 1-2s, now you know you have work to do. If you have an even set, you still have work to do. We recommend completing a scientific-based Emotional Intelligence assessment. At the end of this book, we have a resource list to assess yourself and/or your team.

By understanding and managing our emotions, we become better equipped to empathize with others and prioritize fairness, compassion, and inclusivity in our decision-making process. Emotional intelligence also enables us to recognize the ethical implications of our actions, leading us to prioritize social responsibility. When we understand the potential consequences of our actions, act with accountability and integrity, promote fairness and justice, ensure long-term sustainability, and build trust and reputation, we become responsible agents for positive change in the world.

Developing key skills involved in social management can greatly enhance one's ability to effectively navigate and manage social interactions.

In your corporate career, it can lead to increased promotability.

- In your personal life, it can lead to improved social and personal relationships.

Social Management And Responsibility

- In your entrepreneurial ventures, it can lead to improved growth and expansion because you make better connections with clients.

Here are some ways these skills can enhance social management abilities:

1. **Improved Communication:** Effective communication skills enable individuals to express themselves clearly, listen actively, and understand others' perspectives. This leads to better understanding, collaboration, and the ability to resolve conflicts more effectively.

2. **Conflict Resolution:** Developing skills in conflict resolution allows individuals to identify and address conflicts in a constructive manner. They can find common ground, negotiate mutually beneficial solutions, and maintain positive relationships, even in challenging situations.

3. **Enhanced Emotional Intelligence:** Emotional intelligence involves recognizing and managing one's own emotions as well as understanding and empathizing with the emotions of others. By developing emotional intelligence, individuals can better navigate social dynamics, build rapport, and respond empathetically to the needs and feelings of others.

4. **Improved Active Listening:** Active listening skills enable individuals to fully concentrate on and comprehend what others say. This enhances understanding, fosters stronger connections, and allows for more effective communication and problem-solving.

5. **Strengthened Empathy:** Cultivating empathy helps individuals understand and share the feelings and experiences

of others. This promotes understanding, compassion, and the ability to navigate social situations with sensitivity and care.

6. **Effective Problem-Solving:** Developing problem-solving skills equips individuals with the ability to analyze situations, identify potential solutions, and make informed decisions. This allows for more effective resolution of social challenges and the ability to find creative solutions.

7. **Assertiveness:** Being assertive involves expressing thoughts, feelings, and needs in a respectful and confident manner. Developing assertiveness enables individuals to communicate their boundaries, advocate for themselves, and build stronger relationships based on mutual respect.

8. **Adaptability:** Social management often requires individuals to navigate through diverse social situations and personalities. Developing adaptability skills allows individuals to adjust to different contexts, understand and respect cultural differences, and effectively engage with a variety of people.

9. **Leadership:** Leadership skills are crucial in social management as they enable individuals to inspire, motivate, and guide others towards common goals. Developing leadership abilities enhances one's ability to influence and positively impacts social dynamics.

10. **Resilience:** Social management can be challenging at times and setbacks are inevitable. Building resilience allows individuals to bounce back from setbacks, maintain a positive attitude, and persevere in the face of adversity.

By developing these skills, individuals can enhance their social management abilities, build stronger relationships, foster positive social dynamics, and create a harmonious and productive social environment.

Social Management And Responsibility

Social management and responsibility are essential aspects of emotional intelligence. Building rapport, responding instead of reacting, showing gratitude, setting boundaries, and having conflict resolution and negotiation skills can contribute to effective social management. Understanding the ethical implications of our actions and prioritizing social responsibility are important for making ethical choices and creating a positive impact on individuals and society. By embracing emotional intelligence, we can build stronger relationships, foster a healthier workplace, and contribute to a more ethical and socially responsible world.

CHAPTER 6

GAINING CONTROL OF OUR EMOTIONS

> *Employees who believe that their leaders treat them with respect are 55% more engaged, 63% more satisfied, and 58% more focused on their jobs.*

Emotional intelligence is not just about understanding and managing emotions but also about gaining control over them. In this chapter, we explore the many ways in which we can gain control over our emotions, allowing us to respond more effectively to challenging situations.

Understanding Emotions

Most social scientists agree that there are seven emotional expressions that are basic to every culture. The thing to keep in mind is that our face often displays more than one emotion at a time, so we will witness things like a person smiling, although their eyes are sad.

According to Dr. Paul Ekman, a renowned psychologist, we can teach people how to recognize these emotions (as well as hidden emotions) by carefully reading what is shown on someone's face. The seven emotions and their telltale signs are as follows.

Sadness

Sadness comes with a set of identifiable marks where the eyebrows are drawn upwards in the middle and curve down towards the end. There is also a slight vertical furrow between the eyes. Taken together, this is called Darwin's grief muscle. The mouth pointed downward similarly, with the outside corners of the mouth pointing downward.

Anger

When we are angry, we often press our lips together so hard that the upper lip almost disappears. The eyes may widen across the upper eyelids, and the lower eyelids are contracted. The inner corners of the eyebrows pull downward, and there is often enough pressure to create a furrowed brow.

Fear

In fear, a scared person's eyebrows may be close to horizontal and wrinkles in evidence across the forehead. Like anger, people who are frightened may open the upper eyelid more widely and show more of the whites of their eyes, while the corners of their mouths pull the lips into a horizontal line.

Happiness

Happiness is generally accompanied by rising cheeks, and we describe the accompanying smile as going up to someone's eyes when the muscles around the eyes tighten (hence, the way that smile lines lead to permanent lines around the eyes). Authentic smiles, also called a Duchenne smile, were first described by French neurologist Guillaume Benjamin Amand Duchenne de Boulogne. They are characterized by eye wrinkles, whereas a phony or forced smile is missing characteristic smile lines.

Surprise

Raised upper eyelids, in addition to exposing additional whites of the eye, are often accompanied by surprise. The mouth or jaw may also open as a part of the response.

Contempt

Is anyone rolling their eyes at you? This gesture is quite common in expressions of contempt, in addition to the left corner of the lip being pulled out asymmetrically, creating a dimple.

Disgust

People who feel disgusted may wrinkle their nose as they might to an unpleasant smell, and/or generate wrinkles at the top of the nose between their eyes. The upper lip may also be raised.

What Do Emotions Tell Us?

Emotion	What It Tells Us
Sadness	Lost something of value
Anger	The way is blocked or get out of my way
Fear	Possible threat – be prepared
Happiness	Gained something of value, the way is safe
Surprise	Something unexpected happened
Contempt	Not worthy of care, hardening of feelings
Disgust	Rules are violated

Applying Emotional Intelligence

Emotional expressions do not tell us the cause that prompts the response. You have to take into account the situation in which the emotion is expressed and how your own emotions affect the situation in order to understand it. As you try to understand emotions that you witness, it is important to remember that emotions in themselves are neither positive nor negative; it is what we do with the emotion that creates the outcome.

Below are some examples of both a positive and negative use of each emotion.

	Positive Use	**Negative Use**
Sadness	A positive use of **sadness** is it lets people know that you need help. On many work teams people take care of others who have gone through a negative experience. (Failed project, failed to meet a team goal).	A negative use of **sadness** is when people don't manage or acknowledge it and it turns into depression.
Anger	A positive use of **anger** is when someone uses the emotion to catalyze a cause. It was anger over discrimination that spurred reforms.	A negative use of **anger** is when people hurt others through physical violence and verbal abuse.

	Positive Use	**Negative Use**
Fear	A positive use of **fear** is when people spend more time preparing for an event because they fear the consequences.	A negative use of **fear** is when people don't act or don't live a fulfilled life because they fear failure. Someone doesn't apply for promotion because they fear they are not ready.
Happiness	A positive use of **happiness** is the positive effect it has on connecting people.	A negative use of **happiness** is when people ignore responsibilities because they are more interested in having fun. They socialize at work more than they are exceeding expectations.
Surprise	A positive use of **surprise** is creating excitement for a new product, project, service.	A negative use of **surprise** is not informing people around changes that affect their livelihood, their responsibilities. A leader withholding critical information.

	Positive Use	**Negative Use**
Contempt	A positive use of **contempt** is when people see the consequences of crime or socially unaccepted behavior.	A negative use of **contempt** is a form of bullying to negatively influence others.
Disgust	A positive use of **disgust** (similar to contempt) is to inform people of unacceptable behavior.	A negative use of **disgust** is when it is used to hurt others in a social situation.

A Box Full of Kisses

Some time ago, a man punished his 3-year-old daughter for wasting a roll of gold wrapping paper. Money was tight, and he became infuriated when the child tried to decorate a box to put under the Christmas tree.

Nevertheless, the little girl brought the gift to her father the next morning and said, "This is for you, Daddy."

The man became embarrassed by his earlier overreaction, but his rage continued when he saw that the box was empty. He yelled at her; "Don't you know, when you give someone a present, there is supposed to be something inside?"

The little girl looked up at him with tears in her eyes and cried.

"Oh, Daddy, it's not empty at all. I blew kisses into the box. They're all for you, Daddy."

The father was crushed. He put his arms around his little girl and begged for forgiveness. A short time later, an accident took the life of the child. Her father kept the gold box by his bed for many years, and whenever he was discouraged, he would take out an imaginary kiss and remember the love of the child who had put it there.

Moral of the story: *Love is the most precious gift in the world. As a leader, you must learn how to control your emotions, feelings, and words, because once they are out, it is hard to pull them back.*

The Feelings Wheel

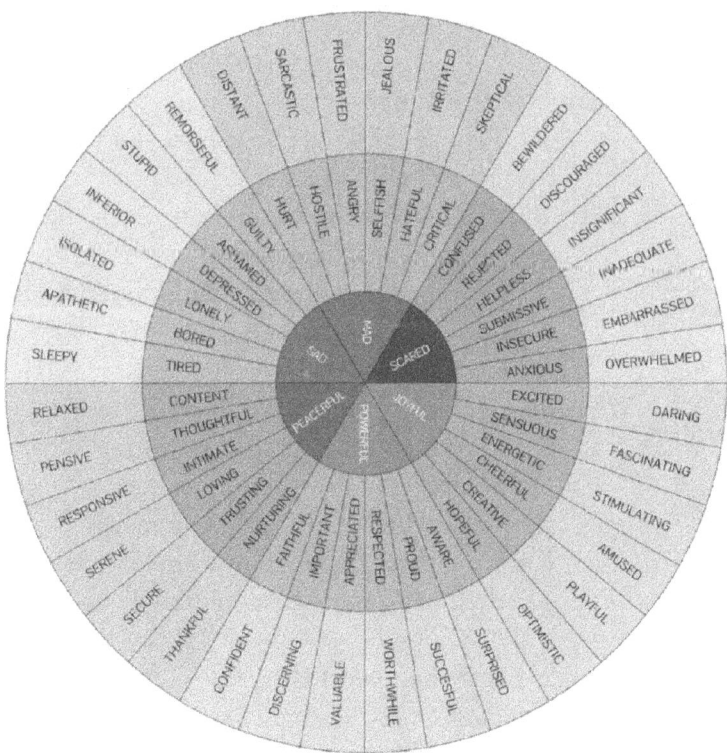

How to use The Feeling Wheel

1. Take out The Feeling Wheel when you want to explore the emotions you are experiencing.
2. Begin with more general emotions in the center of the wheel, for example, sad or mad.
3. Move towards the outer emotions and identify the specific emotions you are feeling.
4. Accept the emotional experience and self-reflect.
5. If you wish, communicate your emotions to others in a healthy way.

To Better Understand the Emotion, You Are Feeling: ASK

1. **What am I thinking?**
    a. You may be thinking about how you will fail in the big project tomorrow.
    b. You may be thinking about how much you hate your job and boss/teammates.
        o Negative thoughts can cause negative emotions.

2. **What do I feel in my body?**
    a. Do you feel your face getting hot?
    b. Do you feel your heart beating faster?
    c. Do you feel butterflies in your stomach?
    d. Knowing these signals allows you to know that you need to do something to calm down.

3. **How do I act when I feel this way?**
    a. Am I arguing or yelling?
    b. Am I shutting down and refusing to talk?
    c. Am I avoiding an important task?

d. Your actions can be a key signal letting you know that your emotions are rising, and it is time to use your coping skills.

Coping Skills (4 categories)

1. **Relaxation Skills**: Things you can do to relax your brain and body.
2. **Distraction Skills:** Things you can do to get your mind off of your stressful emotions.
3. It is not to avoid it; it is just to give yourself time to relax and revisit it later when you are calm and under control.
4. **Movement Skills:** Things you can do to move your body to physically release stressful emotions.
5. **Thinking Skills:** These can be encouraging statements you say to yourself or questions you ask yourself to challenge your negative thoughts.

Developing coping strategies is crucial in managing emotional triggers. Engaging in self-care activities, seeking support from trusted friends or professionals, practicing relaxation techniques, and using positive self-talk are all effective ways to cope with triggers. It is important to experiment with different strategies to find what works best for us.

If certain triggers consistently overwhelm us or significantly impact our daily lives, seeking professional help from a therapist or counselor can be beneficial. They can provide guidance and support in managing triggers and developing effective coping strategies.

Journaling Can Be Powerful

Once you have identified your emotions, it is time for you to move on. Journaling is a powerful tool for gaining control over emotions. Journaling provides a safe and private space for self-reflection and emotional regulation. By expressing and reflecting on our thoughts and emotions in a journal, we can gain clarity about what we are experiencing and why. This process promotes self-awareness and helps us identify patterns in our behaviors and interactions with others. Journaling also allows us to track our personal growth and progress over time, thus providing a sense of clarity and direction.

There are several ways in which journaling can be used for self-reflection and emotional regulation. First, journaling allows for emotional expression. By writing down our thoughts and feelings, we can release pent-up emotions, process challenging situations, and better understand the root causes of our emotions. This emotional expression promotes self-awareness and helps to regulate intense emotions.

Second, journaling encourages self-reflection. By writing about our experiences, we gain a deeper understanding of ourselves, our values, and our goals. We can reflect on our successes, challenges, and areas for growth. This self-reflection helps us identify patterns, gain insight into our behaviors and choices, and make positive changes in our lives.

Journaling also serves as a problem-solving tool. By writing about a specific issue or dilemma, we can brainstorm possible solutions, evaluate different perspectives, and make informed decisions. This process of problem-solving through journaling enhances our critical thinking skills, promotes emotional regulation, and reduces stress and anxiety.

Gaining Control Of Our Emotions

Incorporating gratitude journaling into our practice can shift our focus towards positive emotions and experiences. By regularly writing about things, we are grateful for, we train our minds to notice and appreciate the good things in life. This cultivates a positive mindset, increases optimism, and improves emotional wellbeing. Gratitude journaling also serves as a reminder of the positive aspects amidst challenging times, aiding in emotional regulation and resilience.

Furthermore, journaling allows us to track our progress and growth over time. By periodically reviewing our past entries, we can see how far we have come, identify patterns of growth, and celebrate our successes. This reflection on personal progress boosts self-confidence and motivation, reinforcing emotional regulation and resilience.

Lastly, journaling can serve as a form of release and letting go. By writing about challenging or painful experiences, we can acknowledge and validate our emotions, gain perspective, and find closure. This process can be cathartic and help us move forward with a sense of emotional release and relief.

In addition to journaling, meditation and mindfulness practices can also help us gain control over our emotions. Breath awareness meditation, body scan meditation, loving-kindness meditation, mindful walking, mindful eating, and noting or labeling emotions are all powerful techniques that promote present-moment awareness, calm the mind, and regulate emotions.

To order your personal copy of The Emotional Intelligence Journal visit LaFleur Leadership Institute or Trendy Elite Coaching.

Developing self-awareness is another crucial step in gaining control over emotions. By paying attention to our emotions and their triggers, we can identify patterns and understand why certain situations have such a powerful impact on our emotions. Reflecting on past experiences that have caused strong emotional reactions can provide insights into our triggers and help us respond more effectively.

Self-awareness is one of the most important ways to improving your emotional intelligence. We recommend the following questions to gain greater self-awareness. Spend time evaluating, contemplating, and thinking through your life's journey, both personally and professionally. Before writing this book, we spent time thinking about questions 1-4.

Self-awareness questions on values and life goals

1. What does your ideal "you" look like?
2. What kinds of dreams and goals do you have?
3. Why are these dreams or goals important?
4. What keeps you from these dreams or goals?
5. Rank 5-10 of the most important things in your life in your career, family, relationships, love, money, and so on.
6. Now, consider the proportion of time you dedicate to each of these things.
7. What would you recommend to your children to do or not do?

Once you have done this for your personal life, answer these same questions for your professional life.

1. What does your ideal "career/position" look like?
2. What kinds of dreams and goals do you have?
3. Why are these dreams or goals important to you?
4. What is stopping you from these dreams or goals?

Gaining Control Of Our Emotions

5. Rank 5-10 of the most important things in your career, leadership, and entrepreneurship.
6. Now, consider the proportion of time you dedicate to each of these things.
7. What would you recommend to your employee (team) to do or not do?

There are several ways to improve your self-awareness. You should consider completing the DISC/EIQ Combo Assessment and VIA Strength Assessment.

The DISC/EIQ Combo assessment is designed not only to help you become more self-aware but also to help you increase your personal and professional success by becoming aware of your personality profile and emotional intelligence.
- To secure your DISC/EIQ assessment, contact LaFleur Leadership Institute or Trendy Elite Coaching for immediate access.

The VIA Strength Assessment will help you identify your 24 core strengths. Character strengths are different from your other personal strengths, such as your unique skills, talents, interests, and resources, because they reflect the "real" you—who you are at your core. Every individual possesses **all 24 character strengths** in different degrees, giving each person a unique character strengths profile. Discover your personal character strengths profile by taking the scientifically validated **VIA Survey**.
- Both the Adult Strength Survey and Youth Strength Survey can be found on the LaFleur Leadership Institute website.

You may ask, so now that I have completed these assessments, what do I do with this information? This is time for you to get with a coach. We can offer these services to help you review your results and the next steps.

If you want your team to complete one or both assessments, contact us via our website so that we can facilitate a team workshop.

*There was once a little boy who had a very bad temper. His father decided to hand him a bag of nails and said that every time the boy lost his temper, he had to hammer a nail into the fence. On the first day, the boy hammered **37 nails** into the fence.*

The boy gradually began to **control his temper** over the next few weeks, and the number of nails he was hammering in the fence slowly decreased. He discovered that it was easier to control his temper than hammer the nails into the fence. Finally, the day came when the boy did not lose his temper. He told his father the news, and the father suggested that the boy should now pull out a nail every day he kept his temper under control.

The days passed, and the young boy was finally able to tell his father that all the nails were gone. The father took his son by the hand and led him to the fence.

"You have done well, my son, but look at the holes in the fence. The fence will never be the same. When you say things in anger, they leave a scar just like this one. You can put a knife in a man and draw it out. It won't matter how many times you say I'm sorry, the wound is still there."

Moral of the story: *Control your anger, and do not say things to people in the heat of the moment, **that you may later regret**. Some things in life, you are unable to take back.*

Gaining Control Of Our Emotions

Noticing the physical sensations that arise when we are triggered is also important. Emotions often manifest as bodily sensations, and by becoming aware of these cues, we can intervene before the emotional response escalates.

Practicing mindfulness allows us to observe our thoughts, emotions, and bodily sensations without judgment. By cultivating present-moment awareness, we create a space for intentional response instead of impulsive reaction.

Challenging assumptions and beliefs is another effective strategy to manage emotional triggers. Sometimes our reactions are based on distorted or unhelpful thinking patterns. We can respond more effectively by examining alternative perspectives and reframing our thoughts.

Gaining control over our emotions is an essential aspect of emotional intelligence. Journaling, meditation, mindfulness, self-awareness, challenging assumptions, and developing coping strategies are all powerful tools that can help us respond more effectively to challenging situations. By incorporating these practices into our lives, we can cultivate emotional regulation, resilience, and a greater sense of control over our emotions.

CHAPTER 7
ENHANCING EMOTIONAL INTELLIGENCE WITH ARTIFICIAL INTELLIGENCE

> 61% of employers are more likely to promote workers with high emotional intelligence over candidates with high IQ.

Emotional intelligence requires not just understanding but mastery over our emotions. Artificial intelligence (AI) offers tools that augment these capabilities, enhancing both personal and organizational emotional dynamics. While Emotional intelligence enables individuals to effectively manage and understand their own and others' emotions, AI offers tools that augment these capabilities, providing deep insights into human emotions and their impact on behavior. Our emotions are like waves of the ocean—sometimes calm and sometimes turbulent. Navigating them requires the discipline and training of a muscle, constantly honed for resilience and adaptability.

In this new era, the blending of AI with emotional intelligence is altering our approach to these emotional voyages. AI does not just support emotional intelligence; it expands its reach and depth, offering tools that provide insights to refine both personal and organizational emotional dynamics.

Tools to Regulate Your Emotions with AI Support

Effectively regulating emotions is central to enhancing emotional intelligence. Various tools and techniques, including those powered by AI, can assist in better managing one's emotional landscape:

1. **Self-Awareness Exercises:** Mindfulness and reflection are key in recognizing one's emotional states. AI-enhanced apps further track mood fluctuations to identify patterns and triggers in mood changes and suggest activities based on these emotional responses, fostering deeper self-awareness.

2. **Smart Watches and Fitness Trackers:** These devices help users become more aware of their physical responses to stress or emotional turmoil. AI will analyze the data to provide feedback on maintaining calmness and balance.

3. **Emotional Vocabulary Enhancement:** AI-driven language learning tools can help individuals expand their emotional vocabulary, allowing for more precise expression and understanding of feelings. They also bridge cultural gaps in expression and understanding. For instance, in a multinational corporation, these tools have been instrumental in training employees to recognize and respect the nuanced emotional expressions of their colleagues from different cultural backgrounds.

4. **Journaling and Feedback:** Digital journaling platforms use AI to analyze emotional patterns and provide feedback, helping users identify triggers and manage their emotional responses more effectively. By employing predictive analytics, these platforms can

forecast potential emotional triggers based on historical data, allowing users to proactively plan strategies for managing future emotional challenges.

5. **Real-time Emotional Analysis:** AI technologies in workplaces or educational settings analyze speech patterns and facial expressions to provide real-time insights into the emotional climate, aiding leaders in making informed decisions that enhance group dynamics.

6. **Customized Learning Environments:** AI can offer interactive learning modules that adapt based on the user's progress in developing self-awareness. These platforms may include scenarios or simulations where users must identify emotions correctly or choose responses based on their understanding of emotional cues.

Benefits of Integrating AI with Emotional Intelligence

By merging the intuitive grasp of emotional intelligence with AI's analytical capabilities, we enhance our ability to interact empathetically and respond effectively in diverse contexts.

- **Increased Understanding of Emotions:** AI can uncover patterns in emotional data, providing individuals with a deeper understanding of their emotional triggers and responses.

- **Efficiency:** AI can process emotional data quickly and at a scale, allowing for real-time responsiveness. This real-time feedback enhances the effectiveness and efficiency in environments like customer service or mental health support.

- **Personalization:** Tailored interactions based on an individual's emotional state, enhancing engagement and effectiveness.

- **Enhanced Decision-Making:** AI can be used in strategic decision-making by understanding emotional patterns.

- **Accessibility:** AI tools can make emotional intelligence insights more accessible to a wider audience. People in remote areas or with limited resources can access AI-driven emotional intelligence support through apps and online platforms. Additionally, the 24/7 availability of AI tools ensures that emotional support is accessible at any time, overcoming limitations related to time zones or the availability of human professionals.

For instance, in the realm of mental health, a workplace wellness startup developed an AI-powered app to monitor users' text inputs and voice logs to detect signs of mental health issues such as stress, anxiety, or depression.

Outcome: The app provides users with personalized reports and recommendations, such as engaging in specific mindfulness activities, contacting a therapist, or adjusting their work schedule. Employers using this app noted a decrease in reported stress levels among employees and improved overall productivity.

Ethical Considerations in AI for Enhancing Emotional Intelligence

As we embrace the power of AI to augment emotional intelligence, we must carefully navigate the ethical complexities that arise. The potential for AI to deeply understand and influence human emotions places a great responsibility on developers and users alike to ensure that these technologies are used in ways that respect individual dignity and promote genuine well-being.

Key ethical considerations include:

- **Privacy Concerns:** The use of AI in analyzing emotional data raises significant privacy issues. It is vital to ensure that individuals' emotional data is collected, stored, and used in a manner that respects their privacy and is in accordance with legal standards.

- **Bias and Fairness:** AI systems are only as unbiased as the data they are trained on. If the data contains inherent biases, the AI's interpretation of emotions could be skewed, leading to unfair or harmful outcomes.

- **Emotional Manipulation:** There exists a potential for AI systems equipped with emotional intelligence capabilities to manipulate emotions and decisions. Establishing ethical guidelines and regulatory measures is essential for avoiding such misuse.

Real World Case Study: Keeping Patient Data Secure

A healthcare provider implemented an AI-driven system to monitor patients' emotions and adjust treatment approaches accordingly. Although this technology significantly improved personalized care, it raised privacy concerns as sensitive emotional data were collected and analyzed. To address these issues, the provider implemented strict data encryption, gained explicit consent from patients, and conducted regular audits to ensure compliance with privacy regulations. Additionally, the AI system was trained on a diverse dataset to minimize biases and ensure fair treatment across different demographic groups.

Summary

The integration of AI with emotional intelligence offers transformative potential for personal growth and leadership enhancement. By leveraging AI, individuals can gain deeper insights into their emotions and those of others, thereby enabling more empathetic and effective communication.

Practical Application

Sam had always faced challenges in managing emotions, from meeting tight deadlines at work to navigating conflicts with friends. An unsettling disagreement with a close friend highlighted the need for a change. During this time, Sam came across an article discussing emotional intelligence that opened his eyes to a different perspective.

Interested by the concept of navigating emotions, Sam began to use an AI-powered journaling app to document moments of emotional distress and insight. This app used sentiment analysis to highlight patterns in Sam's emotional responses, offering personalized prompts and strategies to cope with challenging situations.

As Sam delved deeper into self-improvement, mindfulness emerged as a key tool. An AI-driven mindfulness app provided guided meditation sessions, adapting the content based on Sam's current emotional state, detected through voice and

Enhancing Emotional Intelligence With Artificial Intelligence

facial expression analysis. Initially challenging, meditation soon became a source of clarity and calm amid the emotional turmoil.

When a major project fell apart because of a colleague's oversight, Sam's instinctive reaction was to assign blame and express frustration. However, armed with insights from his AI-enhanced emotional intelligence training, Sam paused to collect his thoughts and discussed recovery options with patience and empathy. This approach led to constructive dialogue and a cohesive plan to move forward.

In the following weeks, colleagues noticed a positive change in Sam's approach, and the storms of life became more manageable. This transformation inspired others, showing the profound impact of integrating emotional intelligence with AI tools.

The moral of the story is clear: Developing emotional intelligence, especially when augmented by AI, can lead to transformative personal and professional growth. By leveraging AI tools to enhance emotional regulation and self-awareness, individuals can elevate their leadership capabilities, improve their interactions with others, and positively influence their professional environments.

As leaders, we must prioritize and practice the use of these emotional regulation techniques in our personal lives and professional roles. By embracing emotional intelligence, leaders can foster impactful changes both within us and throughout our teams, ultimately creating a more supportive and effective leadership approach.

Reflection Questions:

1. How can AI-powered tools enhance your ability to recognize and manage your own emotions? Reflecting on how technology such as sentiment analysis and personalized prompts can be integrated into your daily routine to help you better understand your emotional patterns.
2. How can mindfulness and meditation, supported by AI, transform your approach to stressful situations? Think about how AI-driven personalization of mindfulness practices could impact your ability to remain calm and focused under pressure.
3. How might developing your emotional intelligence with AI tools change your interactions and relationships and what specific steps can you take to apply these tools effectively?
4. How might the example of Sam inspire you to apply emotional intelligence and AI to your leadership or personal development journey? Find aspects of Sam's story that resonate with you, and how you can incorporate similar strategies into your own life to achieve growth and transformation.

PART III:
MASTERING EMOTIONAL INTELLIGENCE FOR BUSINESS SUCCESS

CHAPTER 8

NAVIGATING ONLINE RELATIONSHIPS

> *95% of surveyed HR managers and 99% of employees believe that emotional intelligence is a must-have skill for every staff member.*

Imagine stepping into a virtual conference room filled with team members from every corner of the globe. Sounds exciting, right? But as a leader striving to implement emotional intelligence online, you soon realize the complexities are far greater than the initial thrill. One of the challenges is allowing genuine emotional connection through a screen. Unlike face-to-face interactions, where body language, tone, and timely responses play pivotal roles in conveying empathy and understanding, the digital realm tends to diminish emotional nuance. The lack of physical cues can make it harder to read between the lines, understand stress, or offer timely support. This can turn a seemingly straightforward meeting into an emotionally distant transaction.

This chapter explores how emotional intelligence can be leveraged to foster positive interactions and navigate the complexities of online relationships in both personal and professional contexts.

Understanding Online Relationships

Online relationships, whether personal or professional, present unique challenges and opportunities that differ from traditional, offline interactions. Without the ability to see body language, hear tone of voice, or see facial expressions, it becomes difficult to fully understand the emotions and intentions of others. A challenge in the online space is the delayed response times that often go with online communication. The asynchronous nature of digital platforms means that messages can go unanswered for hours or even days, which can be misinterpreted as disinterest or avoidance. This delay in response can create tension and uncertainty, further complicating the dynamics of online relationships. Another consideration is the overloading of communication from various channels simultaneously. This constant flow of communication from multiple places (chat, email, virtual meetings, social media, etc.) makes it challenging to maintain meaningful interactions and give conversations the attention they need.

In the online world, written communications are permanent. Unlike spoken words, which disappear in thin air, written messages can be revisited and scrutinized, potentially leading to long-term consequences. This permanence adds a layer of pressure to online interactions, as one must carefully consider their words before hitting the send button.

This is where emotional intelligence plays a pivotal role in interpreting messages accurately and responding empathetically.

The Role of Emotional Intelligence in Online Relationships

Emotional intelligence in digital environments involves understanding and managing one's own emotions and effectively interpreting others' emotional cues, even when they are conveyed through text. This skill set is crucial to building trust and rapport in online relationships.

Navigating Online Relationships

Building Trust Online

1. *Consistency in Communication*
Being consistent in how and when you communicate can build trust. Regular updates, predictable response times, and a steady communication style reassure others of your reliability and commitment to the relationship.

How can you enhance your team's confidence in your leadership through consistent communication?

2. *Transparency and Honesty*
Clear and open communication is key to building trust online. Sharing your thoughts and feelings transparently, while respecting the other person's views, fosters a deeper connection.

How might increased transparency in your interactions deepen trust among team members?

3. *Privacy and Discretion*
Respecting privacy in digital communication is crucial. Being cautious about what personal information you share and respecting the boundaries of others enhances trust.

What steps can you take to ensure privacy and foster trust?

Managing Misunderstandings

Misunderstandings are common in online communication because of the lack of contextual cues. To effectively manage these:

1. *Seek Clarification*
When a message is unclear, ask for clarification instead of making assumptions. This helps avoid the escalation of potential conflicts.

How can you implement this approach to prevent potential conflicts?

2. *Assume Positive Intent*
Always assuming positive intent can prevent many conflicts from arising. This approach encourages giving the benefit of the doubt when interpreting ambiguous messages.

What impact could this mindset have on your team dynamics?

3. *Apologize When Necessary*
If a misunderstanding occurs, a sincere apology can go a long way towards mending the relationship. Acknowledging your part in a misunderstanding shows your maturity and respect for the relationship.

Can you recall a situation where an apology improved a professional relationship?

Enhancing Connectivity in Professional Relationships

In a professional setting, digital emotional intelligence can enhance collaboration and team dynamics, especially in remote work environments.

1. *Regular Virtual Meetings*
Regular video calls can help maintain a sense of team presence and cohesion. Seeing team members face-to-face, even virtually, can reinforce connections and facilitate better emotional understanding.

How regularly do you engage with your team visually?

2. *Shared Digital Spaces*

Creating shared digital spaces for informal interactions such as virtual coffee breaks or social media groups can mimic the watercooler conversations of physical offices and build camaraderie.

What virtual activities could you introduce to enhance your team bonding?

3. *Recognition and Feedback*
Providing prompt and constructive feedback, as well as recognizing achievements, can boost morale and maintain a positive team dynamic. Always deliver feedback with consideration for the recipient's feelings and perspective.

How can you better recognize and motivate your team remotely?

Sustaining Personal Relationships Online

Maintaining personal relationships online requires effort and emotional awareness, particularly in managing long-distance friendships or family ties.

1. *Regular Communication*
Schedule regular check-ins and updates. Consistent interaction helps keep the relationship vibrant and allows for sharing emotions and daily experiences.

2. *Celebrate Special Occasions*
Utilizing digital tools to celebrate birthdays, anniversaries, or major achievements together can help sustain the emotional connection, making the distance feel smaller.

What creative digital celebrations could you organize?

3. *Digital Dates and Activities*
Plan activities that can be done together online, such as watching a movie through a streaming service or playing online games. These shared experiences can create memories and strengthen bonds.

What activities could you plan that resonate with your relationships?

Case Study: Online Support Groups for Emotional Sharing

In this digital era, support groups for mental health have evolved from face-to-face meetings to virtual platforms, presenting unique challenges in fostering genuine connections. These virtual support groups are crucial for individuals to share experiences and feelings in a supportive environment despite never meeting in person.

To facilitate these interactions, various online platforms provide moderated chat rooms, forums, and video calls. The design of these platforms is intentional, ensuring that every participant feels secure regarding their vulnerability. The facilitators of these groups are trained in emotional intelligence to effectively guide discussions, ensuring that each participant feels heard. This is vital in a setting where nonverbal cues are absent and misunderstandings can easily occur. The outcome of integrating emotional intelligence into these groups has been overwhelmingly positive. Participants reported feeling less isolated and more understood, with many experiencing significant improvements in their mental health. The consistent emotional support and validation have fostered a strong sense of community and understanding among members.

These online support groups offer valuable lessons and insights that can be broadly applied to enhance online interactions and relationships. Reflecting on their success, here are practical steps to consider for those looking to improve their own digital communications:

Reflective Steps:

1. Assess Your Current Online Communication Style
- Reflect on how consistently and transparently you communicate. Are there areas where you can improve your respect for privacy or clarity in conveying your emotions?

2. Implement Regular Check-Ins
- Regular virtual meetings or calls can help maintain and enhance connections in professional settings or personal relationships. How can you better schedule these interactions to foster understanding?

3. Use Technology to Your Advantage
- Digital tools, such as real-time translation and shared spaces, can significantly enhance online communication and emotional intelligence. Which tools could you integrate into your practices to support emotional clarity?

4. Prioritize Emotional Clarity
- In the absence of physical presence, clear and emotive language, along with multimedia elements, can help convey feelings more accurately and reduce misunderstandings.

5. **Foster a Culture of Feedback**
   - Encourage and normalize the provision of constructive feedback in all your interactions to maintain a positive dynamic and continuously improve communication skills.

6. **Celebrate Milestones Digitally**
   - Use digital platforms to celebrate personal and professional milestones through digital means to maintain morale and foster team spirit

Quick Tips for Navigating Online Relationships

Tip	Description
Consistency in Communication	Maintain regular updates, predictable response times, and a steady communication style to build trust.
Transparency and Honesty	Share thoughts and feelings openly and respectfully to foster deeper connections.
Privacy and Discretion	Be cautious about sharing personal information and respect others' boundaries to enhance trust.
Seek Clarification	Ask for clarification when a message is unclear to avoid misunderstandings.
Assume Positive Intent	Give the benefit of the doubt when interpreting ambiguous messages to prevent conflicts.

Navigating Online Relationships

Tip	Description
Apologize When Necessary	Offer sincere apologies to mend relationships and show maturity and respect.
Regular Virtual Meetings	Schedule consistent video calls to maintain team presence and emotional understanding.
Shared Digital Spaces	Create informal digital spaces for team interactions to build camaraderie.
Recognition and Feedback	Provide timely and constructive feedback to boost morale and maintain a positive team dynamic.
Regular Communication	Schedule consistent check-ins and updates to keep personal relationships vibrant.
Celebrate Special Occasions	Use digital tools to celebrate special occasions and sustain emotional connections.
Digital Dates and Activities	Plan online activities like streaming movies or playing games together to create shared experiences.
Emotive Language	Use clear language to express feelings and reduce ambiguity in messages.
Use of Emojis and Multimedia	Incorporate emojis, GIFs, and images to add emotional expression to text communications.
Tone and Pacing	Pay attention to the tone and pacing of messages to convey emotional context effectively.

CHAPTER 9

EMOTIONAL INTELLIGENCE IN BUSINESS PRACTICES

> *Demands for emotional intelligence skills across all industries are expected to grow by 26% in the US and 22% in Europe by 2030. The market is driven by the increasing awareness among organizations about the benefits of emotional intelligence.*

This is a great story about the use of emotional intelligence.

"Once at an executive leadership conference in New York, Linda Kaplan Thaler (the lady that came up with the Aflac commercials), spoke for 2 hours.

After the conference ended, she told us about her time with Warren Buffet. She said at the event that you would only get 10 minutes with Mr. Buffet. She said, she studied up all about him in preparation for her 10 minutes with him. She found that Cherry Coke was his favorite drink. He has made millions of dollars with Coke, so no surprise he loves the product. So, as she came into the meeting with him, they reminded her that she had only 10 minutes. As she sat down, she handed him a Cherry Coke and said, "I know I only have 10 minutes, but I figured we would start with your favorite beverage. As he popped the can, he looked at her and said young lady you can have as much time as you want. No

Emotional Intelligence In Business Practices

one has ever started an interview with my favorite beverage, and she spent 1.5 hours with him."

What was she doing? *She understood that connecting was all about others. If you want to connect with others, you have to forget yourself. You have to forget yourself in conversation and you have to forget yourself in speaking, teaching, and leading.*

In the fast-paced world of business, emotional intelligence plays a vital role in customer service. The ability to recognize and manage one's own emotions as well as understand the emotions of others is essential for building strong relationships and providing exceptional customer experiences. In this chapter, we explore how emotional intelligence can be applied in customer service and why it is of utmost importance. Whether you are leading in a hospital laboratory, restaurant, automobile dealership, or school system, we must remember that outstanding customer service is the key to success.

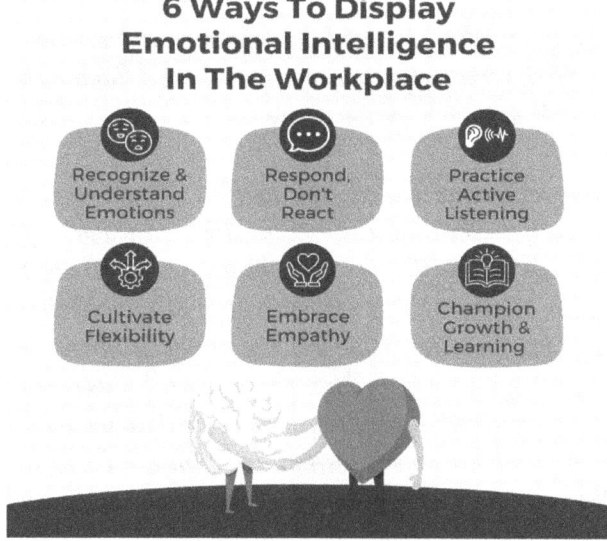

Source: https://www.wellable.co/blog/emotional-intelligence-in-the-workplace/

One of the key aspects of emotional intelligence in customer service is empathy. By empathizing with customers, representatives can connect with them on a deeper level, providing personalized and compassionate support. Empathy involves putting oneself in the customer's position, understanding their wants and needs, and effectively delivering on those needs. This creates a sense of understanding and value for the customer, leading to a more positive and enjoyable interaction.

Active listening is another crucial skill that emotional intelligence brings to customer service. By actively listening to customers, representatives can not only hear their concerns and needs but also understand the emotions behind their words. This allows representatives to respond effectively, address specific needs, and provide appropriate solutions, ultimately leading to greater customer satisfaction.

Emotional regulation is also an important aspect of emotional intelligence in customer service. Interactions with customers can sometimes be challenging or stressful, but emotional intelligence enables representatives to regulate their own emotions and remain calm and composed. By effectively managing their own stress and frustration, representatives can prevent negative emotions from impacting their interactions with customers, ensuring a positive experience.

Conflict resolution is another area where emotional intelligence shines in customer service. Emotional intelligence equips representatives with the skills to handle conflicts and difficult customers. By recognizing and understanding the emotions underlying the conflict, representatives can respond empathetically, de-escalate tense situations, and work towards a resolution that satisfies the customer while maintaining a positive relationship.

Emotional Intelligence In Business Practices

Ush Dhanak, CEO at the EQ Academy, put together a good list of seven examples of Emotional Intelligence in the workplace.

The following are some tips on how employees can use emotional intelligence to succeed:

1. **Self-awareness:** Employees should develop self-awareness by recognizing their own emotions and understanding how they affect their performance. They should regularly assess their emotional state and take steps to manage any negative emotions before interacting with customers.

2. **Empathy:** Employees should strive to understand and empathize with customers' emotions and concerns. This involves:
    - Actively listening to their needs.
    - Acknowledging their feelings.
    - Demonstrating understanding.
    - Showing empathy can help build rapport and trust with customers.

3. **Active listening:** Employees should practice active listening, which involves giving full attention to the customer's words, tone, and emotions. They should:
    - Avoid interrupting,
    - Provide verbal cues to show they are engaged (e.g., using phrases like "I understand" or "I hear you").
    - Summarize or paraphrase the customer's concerns to ensure accurate understanding.

4. **Emotional regulation:** Employees need to manage their emotions effectively, especially in challenging

situations. They should learn techniques to stay calm and composed, such as deep breathing exercises or taking short breaks, if needed. This helps employees respond to customers in a professional and positive manner. This shows a positive response to the new initiatives. Having a positive attitude can help display that you understand what your supervisor is asking you to do and that you are willing to do the work to accomplish it.

5. **Adaptability:** Employees should be adaptable and flexible in their approach. Different customers may have varying emotional states, so employees should be prepared to adjust their communication style accordingly. This might involve being more patient with upset customers or using a more upbeat tone for enthusiastic customers.

6. **Conflict resolution:** Employees should be equipped with conflict resolution skills to handle difficult situations. This involves:
    - Staying calm
    - Actively listening to the customer's concerns
    - Offering appropriate solutions or compromises.

Employees should focus on de-escalating conflicts and finding mutually beneficial resolutions.

7. **Continuous learning:** Employees should actively seek feedback and learn from their experiences. They could review past interactions, identify areas for improvement, and seek guidance or training to enhance their emotional intelligence skills. This ongoing learning process helps employees refine their emotional intelligence and deliver better customer service.

Emotional Intelligence In Business Practices

Emotional intelligence is not only a valuable personal attribute but also a critical skill in the workplace. These seven examples highlight how emotional intelligence can positively impact various aspects of work from individual performance to team dynamics and leadership. As organizations recognize the significance of EQ, fostering emotional intelligence among employees becomes a key strategy for success in today's professional world.

Building trust and loyalty is a crucial goal for any business, and emotional intelligence plays a significant role in achieving this. When representatives demonstrate empathy, active listening, and emotional regulation, customers feel understood, valued, and cared for. This creates a positive customer experience and strengthens the relationship between the customer and the company, leading to increased trust and loyalty.

Chick Fila and Mercedez Benz are two companies that come to mind when we think of great customer service.

If people see value in what you do, they will keep coming back for more.

Truett Cathey, founder of fast-food chain Chick-fil-A, held meetings with his top advisors and management. He noticed in one meeting that they were discussing how the company could grow. Ideas were being tossed around and enthusiasm was very high. Their goal was to do whatever it took to make Chick-fil-A bigger. Calmly, Truett said, "Do not worry about getting bigger. When we get better, our customers will make us bigger."

And they did just that by providing the best and fastest customer service in the fast-food industry.

To get bigger, you must get better — at everything, but particularly at your focus in business. Mercedes Benz seized the luxury car market by campaigning on the safety of their cars. Statistics show that their automobiles are very safe. They attracted a high-dollar market of people who not only wanted to drive a very expensive automobile, but also wanted to stay alive while doing it.

If you sell propane gas or products, find the greatest need your customers have by asking great questions and then being the best at it in your community. If you manage a company, decide today that you will be the Ruth's Chris Steakhouse of propane stores.

Adaptability is another key attribute of emotional intelligence in customer service. Representatives with emotional intelligence can quickly assess the emotional state of a customer and adjust their communication style accordingly. This adaptability helps establish rapport and effectively meet the unique needs of each customer.

Emotional intelligence not only benefits customer interactions, but also contributes to a positive work environment. When representatives practice emotional intelligence, they create a supportive and collaborative atmosphere within the customer service team. This enhances teamwork, employee satisfaction, and overall performance.

Don't Let Your Frogs (Friends) Discourage You

As a group of frogs was traveling through the woods, two of them fell into a deep pit. When the other frogs crowded around the pit and saw how deep it was, they told the two frogs that there was no hope left for them. However, the two frogs decided to ignore what the others were saying, and they proceeded to try and jump out of the pit.

Despite their efforts, the group of frogs at the top of the pit were still saying that they should just give up. That they would never make it out. Eventually, one of the frogs took heed of what the others were saying, and he gave up, falling to his death. The other frog continued to jump as hard as he could. Again, the crowd of frogs yelled at him to the pain and just die.

He jumped even harder and finally made it out. When he got out, the other frogs said, **"Did you not hear us?"** *The frog explained to them that he was deaf. He thought* **they were encouraging him** the entire time.

Moral of the story: *Your words can have a significant effect on others' lives. Think about what you say before it comes out of your mouth. It might just be the difference between life and death.*

Emotional intelligence in customer service is a powerful tool that enables representatives to empathize with customers, actively listen, regulate their emotions, resolve conflicts, build trust and loyalty, adapt to customer needs, and contribute to a positive work environment. By mastering these skills, representatives can effectively deal with difficult customers, address questions, and build trusting relationships, thus resulting in long-term business success.

CHAPTER 10

THE GLOBAL IMPACT OF EMOTIONAL INTELLIGENCE IN BUSINESS

> *Organizations that value and widely use emotional intelligence are 3.2x more effective at leadership development.*

Emotional intelligence significantly influences business on a global scale, especially in fostering international understanding, cooperation, and collaboration. Today, businesses operate in a highly interconnected and culturally diverse world. In such a landscape, the ability to recognize, understand, and manage emotions—both one's own and those of others—is paramount. Emotional intelligence equips leaders and team members with the skills required to effectively navigate complex interpersonal dynamics and cultural differences. With these skills, individuals are better prepared to show empathy and respect for diverse perspectives, facilitating smoother communication and fostering an inclusive work environment. This understanding lays the foundation for enhancing mutual respect and rapport, which is critical for successful international business operations.

Navigating Humor and Sensitivity Across Cultures

The Global Impact Of Emotional Intelligence In Business

Samantha was recently promoted to the VP of business development for a global consulting firm. In this role, she faced the unique challenge of managing diverse cultures across multiple time zones. Samantha prided herself on her ability to communicate effectively, but she quickly discovered that connecting emotionally with her diverse team was filled with misunderstandings and miscommunications. These issues began to negatively affect the team's productivity and morale.

To manage the team's work across different time zones more effectively, Samantha scheduled regular meetings at hours that were convenient for all team members and rotated meeting times to accommodate different regions. This strategy not only reduced fatigue, but also demonstrated her respect for each team member's time. Additionally, Samantha introduced humor into her communications, using jokes and anecdotes to break the ice and build rapport. Initially, this strategy seemed successful as the team bonded over shared laughter. However, Samantha soon learned a crucial lesson when a joke intended to be harmless was perceived as offensive by some team members. This cultural misinterpretation created a rift that Samantha struggled to mend.

Reflecting on the incident, Samantha realized that humor is a double-edged sword. It can bring the team together or divide it further. In response, Samantha organized cultural sensitivity workshops for herself and her team members. These sessions enhanced cultural awareness and fostered a deeper understanding among team members, facilitating open discussions in which everyone could share their cultural backgrounds and personal experiences. This initiative helped clear up previous miscommunications and rebuild trust.

The key takeaway from Samantha's experience is that managing a global team requires more than logistical coordination, which requires deep respect for and understanding of cultural diversity.

While humor can be a powerful tool for building rapport, it must be used with care, ensuring that it aligns with the diverse cultural values of all team members. Through adaptability, cultural awareness, and a commitment to continuous learning, leaders can navigate the complexities of global leadership and foster a more inclusive and harmonious work environment.

Challenges in Implementing Emotional Intelligence Globally

Implementing emotional intelligence globally presents unique challenges that must be carefully navigated. As organizations expand their reach and operations across borders, they confront cultural, linguistic, and societal differences that can either facilitate or hinder the integration of emotional intelligence practices. A thorough examination of these challenges helps leaders gain a deeper understanding of the intricacies involved in fostering emotional intelligence in diverse and dynamic environments.

Cultural Variations in Emotional Expression

Diverse cultures express and interpret emotions differently. Emotional norms and the rules governing the expression of emotions vary widely between cultures. For example, many Western cultures often encourage expressing emotions openly as a sign of authenticity and transparency. By contrast, East Asian cultures might value restraint and maintain harmony, often leading to more subdued emotional expressions.

These cultural differences in emotional display can lead to misinterpretation, where normal behaviors in one culture may be perceived as excessive or insufficiently expressive in another. For global leaders, understanding these cultural nuances and developing a culturally sensitive approach to emotional intelligence is essential. Leaders must be adept at reading emotional cues within the context of each individual's cultural background, and facilitating an environment in which diverse emotional expressions are acknowledged and respected.

Language Barriers

Language barriers and accessibility issues add a layer of complexity to implementing emotional intelligence globally. Even with a common business language, such as English, non-native speakers may struggle to articulate emotional nuances and interpret the emotional content of communication accurately. This can lead to misunderstandings or the exclusion of valuable input from team members who may be less proficient or confident in the chosen language. Additionally, the accessibility of technology and digital literacy can vary significantly among global participants, affecting their ability to meaningfully engage in online emotional intelligence initiatives. To address these concerns, global implementation should include language support such as translation services or multilingual facilitation, and consider varying levels of digital access and capability. Ensuring that content is translated accurately and reflects the nuanced meanings of the original material is fundamental to the success of global emotional intelligence initiatives. Practices such as using clear, simple language in written communication and creating an inclusive space where all voices can be heard are key to overcoming these barriers and fostering a more emotionally intelligent global team.

Accessibility Issues

Global disparities in access to technology can hinder the widespread application of emotional intelligence principles. Accessibility encompasses both technological access and the ability to engage effectively with the provided content. In many regions, there may be limitations related to internet connectivity, availability of digital devices, and technical literacy. In addition, ensuring that the platforms and content are accessible to individuals with disabilities is paramount. This means adopting universally accepted standards for digital accessibility, such as providing screen reader-compatible text, closed captions for videos, and ensuring that the learning management system is navigable through various devices and internet speeds.

Case Study: Implementing Emotional Intelligence Training in a Global Software Development Company

Code Global, an international software company with teams in the US, India, Brazil, and Germany, looked to enhance project outcomes and team dynamics across diverse geographical locations. To address this challenge, the company introduced an emotional intelligence training program for all team members. With an emphasis on understanding cultural differences in communication styles, emotional expressions, and conflict resolution techniques, the training aimed to foster a more harmonious and productive work environment.

Code Global's solution was to implement a digital platform that provided real-time translation and cultural context notes to aid understanding during virtual meetings. The outcome of this initiative was significant. The introduction of digital tools led to a 30% decrease in project delays and 45% reduction in team conflict. The company also received positive feedback from employees, who highlighted improved job satisfaction and better appreciation of diverse working styles.

This case study shows the impact of prioritizing emotional intelligence in a global context. Through a strategic approach that addressed cultural nuances and provided the necessary tools for effective communication and collaboration, Code Global successfully navigated the challenges of global teamwork, ultimately leading to improved project outcomes and enhanced employee satisfaction.

Practical Tips for Implementing Global Emotional Intelligence Online

Tip #1: Use Technology to Bridge Cultural Gaps

- Utilize AI-based translation and cultural interpretation tools during virtual meetings to ensure clear communication.
    - Example: A virtual team uses real-time translation tools during meetings to ensure that all members, regardless of their native language, can participate equally and understand the subtleties in discussions.

Tip #2: Regular Cross-Cultural Training

- Conduct regular training sessions on cultural awareness and emotional intelligence to help team members recognize and respect different emotional expressions and communication styles.
    - Example: An international research firm holds monthly workshops in which employees share insights about their culture's communication styles and emotional norms, fostering a deeper understanding among colleagues.

The Global Impact Of Emotional Intelligence In Business

Tip #3: Adapt Communication Styles

- Encourage team members to adapt their communication to fit the cultural context of their colleagues.
    - Example: A project manager in the UK learns to provide more direct and detailed feedback when working with her team in Japan, respecting the local preference for clarity and precision to avoid misunderstandings.

In conclusion, the global impact of emotional intelligence is profound, influencing everything, from international business to diplomacy. As we continue to navigate a world in which digital interactions often replace face-to-face communication, the ability to effectively manage and convey emotions across cultures has become increasingly important. By addressing the challenges and leveraging the strategies discussed, we can enhance our global interactions and foster a more emotionally intelligent world.

Practical Application

ShopWorld, a prominent global e-commerce enterprise, recently embarked on a groundbreaking initiative to revolutionize its customer service approach. Recognizing the significance of understanding and catering to customers' cultural and emotional nuances, the company introduced an emotionally intelligent AI system to personalize customer interactions across diverse international markets.

This innovative AI system analyzed customer feedback and communication patterns, harnessing cultural insights and language considerations to tailor responses effectively. The objective was clear: to enhance customer satisfaction on a global scale, while minimizing communication errors and streamlining the resolution of customer issues. The results were a 40% increase in international customer satisfaction scores and a significant improvement in operational efficiency.

Realizing the importance of clear communication and precision in a global context, ShopWorld addressed challenges head-on by taking deliberate measures to ensure effective implementation. From managing time zone differences to mitigating cultural misinterpretations, the company established robust protocols and comprehensive solutions. By instituting flexible meeting schedules and leveraging asynchronous communication tools, ShopWorld ensured that all team members could contribute without the constraints of local time differences. The organization also introduced a protocol for clarifying intentions and verifying understanding in communications, thereby preventing misinterpretations, and fostering a harmonious and culturally responsive environment.

Incorporating these meticulous measures and leveraging technology to embrace cultural and emotional diversity, ShopWorld has not only elevated the standard of international customer service, but also set a precedent for other organizations seeking to navigate the complexities of global commerce with empathy and efficacy. The success of this initiative serves as a testament to the power of emotionally intelligent strategies in fostering trust, loyalty, and unparalleled customer satisfaction across borders.

As organizations continuously strive for excellence in a globalized business landscape, the implementation of emotionally intelligent practices serves as a beacon of innovation and adaptability. It underscores the indispensable role of precision, cultural sensitivity, and earnest effort in building customer relationships and operational efficiency worldwide. This lays the groundwork for sustained success in diverse, dynamic market landscapes.

Reflection Questions:

1. How does your current customer service strategy consider the cultural and individual emotional cues in customer interactions?

2. In what ways can an emotionally intelligent AI system enhance your organization's customer service capabilities, especially in a global context?

Next Steps and Follow-Up Actions to Take:

- Assess how your organization currently incorporates cultural and emotional factors into customer interactions.
- Identify areas where an emotionally intelligent AI system can enhance your customer service strategy.
- Research AI systems that offer personalized and culturally sensitive customer interactions.
- Consider the potential benefits and challenges of integrating this technology into your customer service operations.

By focusing on these strategies and effectively integrating emotional intelligence, organizations can navigate the complex dynamics of global business with greater empathy and success.

CHAPTER 11

UNLOCKING THE POWER OF EMOTIONAL INTELLIGENCE

> *Emotional intelligence accounts for nearly 90% of what sets high performers apart from peers with similar technical skills and knowledge.*

A man started a company and built it into a very large enterprise and was planning to hand over the reins to his son at retirement. One day, he walked through the factory and observed his son angrily berating an employee in front of other employees. He looked at his son and motioned for him to come to his office.

David, he began. I wear two hats around here. I am the boss, and I am your father. Right now, I am going to put my supervisor's hat on. You're fired. You are done here. I will not have that kind of behavior in my company and will not ever tolerate employees being treated that way. I have warned you about this kind of thing before, and you are still doing it. So, I have to let you go.

Then he said, "Now, I am going to put on my father's hat.

After a moment's pause, he continued. Son, I heard you just lost your job. How can I help you?

Unlocking The Power Of Emotional Intelligence

The Point: **Emotionally strong leaders honor their relationships while at the same time guarding against letting others control them, especially in difficult relationships.**

Throughout this book, we have delved into the captivating realm of emotional intelligence and its profound impact on our lives. We have dispelled misconceptions and addressed the challenges that come with developing and applying emotional intelligence. Now, as we bring this chapter to a close, let us reflect on the significance of continuously honing our emotional intelligence and the potential it holds for personal and professional triumph.

Emotional intelligence is far greater than being "nice" or suppressing emotions. It encompasses a complex set of skills that involves understanding and effectively managing emotions, both within us and in others. By educating ourselves about the various components of EI, such as self-awareness, self-regulation, empathy, and social skills, we can dismantle the notion that emotional intelligence is solely about being overly pleasant or stifling our emotions.

A new TalentSmart research found that people with high emotional intelligence make an average of $29,000 per year more than people with low EQs. On average, every point increase in emotional intelligence adds $1,300 to an annual salary.

Another common misconception is that emotional intelligence is a fixed trait that cannot be developed. In reality, emotional intelligence is a skill set that can be cultivated and improved over time. By fostering a growth mindset and providing resources and training programs dedicated to nurturing emotional intelligence skills, we can debunk this misconception while encouraging individuals to continually enhance their emotional intelligence.

However, developing emotional intelligence does come with its challenges. Many struggle with a lack of self-awareness or difficulties in managing their emotions under stress. To overcome these hurdles, it is important to provide individuals with tools for self-reflection, introspection, and emotional regulation. Equipping them with techniques to navigate their own inner world will empower them to overcome these challenges, while enhancing their overall emotional intelligence.

A leader's responsibility is to make sure their team has access to all the tools and resources we provided in this book.

Empathy stands as another crucial component of emotional intelligence; yet limited empathy or an inability to fully understand others' emotions can present difficulties in cultivating stronger connections with those around us. By fostering a culture of inclusivity and respect within our communities, whether personal or professional, we can encourage active listening, perspective-taking, seeking understanding from others, and empathizing with their emotions and viewpoints. Through these efforts, we can overcome this challenge and further enhance our empathy.

Finally, translating emotional intelligence into action can prove to be a difficult task. Emotional intelligence is not merely knowledge; it is the application of that knowledge in real-life situations. To overcome this challenge, it is vital to provide individuals with ample opportunities to practice their emotional intelligence skills. By setting goals and action plans and offering ongoing support, feedback, and coaching, we can help individuals overcome this hurdle and effectively apply emotional intelligence in their daily lives.

The continuous development of emotional intelligence plays a pivotal role in personal and professional success. It enriches self-awareness, emotional regulation, empathy, relationship management, and leadership skills. Individuals with high emotional intelligence exhibit effective communication skills, as well as expertise in collaboration, adaptability, resilience, relationship-building, and decision-making. These qualities contribute to success within the workplace, while opening doors to new opportunities and collaborations.

By prioritizing the development of emotional intelligence within us and committing to its continuous growth, we can improve our relationships with others while enhancing our overall well-being. This commitment also resonates within the professional realm since employers highly value emotional intelligence for its ability to enhance teamwork dynamics while fostering productivity and employee satisfaction—an invaluable asset within any organization.

As we come to the culmination of this chapter—of this exploration—let us embrace the power of emotional intelligence wholeheartedly. Let us embark on a journey that involves unlocking its potential through continuous development, practice, and application of these essential skills. By doing so collectively—as individuals striving for growth—we have the ability to unlock the power of emotions together, thus creating a more harmonious world—one filled with empathy where success flourishes at every turn.

Top 10 Habits to Develop Your Emotional Intelligence

1. **Reflect Daily**: Start introspection daily
2. **Seek Feedback**: From peers & mentors
3. **Develop Coping Strategies**: What helps you reset
4. **Align Core Values**: Understand your core values

5. **Set Clear Goals**: Set your objectives
6. **Practice Active Listening**: Truly listen
7. **Build Strong Networks**: Surround yourself with diverse thinkers
8. **Seek a Mentor**: Get someone who is ahead of you to guide you
9. **Attend a Workshop**: Look for training
10. **Practice, Practice, Practice**: EI gets better with practice

IT'S YOUR TURN NOW:

Now that you have learned how to improve your Emotional Intelligence, it is your turn to start writing about your journey.

1. Order your **Emotional Intelligence Journal**
2. Schedule your individual coaching or team assessment workshop.
3. Share your favorite takeaways from this book

To order your journal, schedule your coaching or team assessment workshops, contact LaFleur Leadership Institute or Trendy Elite Coaching.

_____

_____

_____

_____

_____

Unlocking The Power Of Emotional Intelligence

_____

_____

_____

_____

_____

_____

_____

NOTES

Chapter 1

- Dan Goleman: Emotional Intelligence at Work
- The Emotional Intelligence Network. 6seconds.org
- Ten Ways to Increase Your Emotional Intelligence Developing your EQ skills are essential to professional success today. BY YOUNG ENTREPRENEUR COUNCIL@YEC
- Positive Psychology: https://positivepsychology.com/emotional-intelligence-examples/

Chapter 3

- John Maxwell: Good Leaders Ask Great Questions

Chapter 9

- SQM Customer Service QA Experts. https://www.sqmgroup.com/

Chapter 11

- TalentSmart Research Survey Emotional Intelligence Statistics
- https://gitnux.org/emotional-intelligence-statistics

Notes

Throughout The Book

EQ statistics under each chapter heading:

1. Emotional Intelligence Statistics [Fresh Research] Last Updated December 24, 2023. Written & Summarized by: Jannik Lindner. https://gitnux.org/emotional-intelligence-statistics

ACKNOWLEDGMENTS

We thank our colleagues who shared insights that further enhanced this book. We are grateful for your valuable expertise in emotional intelligence, which enriched the depth and quality of this book.

Cedrick's Acknowledgments: I would like to thank my children, TreKessa and Patrick, for helping me become an emotionally strong parent. I would also like to thank some of my former sales team members for pressing on during my low-EQ days and helping me become a better leader with high emotional intelligence. Mimi, Kasib, Anothny, Bernie, Bill, Alfredo, Shamika, Cheryl, Betina, Nick, Laurie, Scott, and the #1 one Starr. And finally, a special thank you to my new grandson Jose Carlos (JC). I know he will help keep his "Pop" growing and learning.

Tywauna's Acknowledgments: I would like to thank my mom Helen, my first example of a true leader. My husband Martinez for always understanding and supporting me on my leadership journey. All of the people that I mentored and coached over the years, who helped my emotional intelligence skills, continued to grow. Finally, my daughter Brooke, who will be the next generation of movers and shakers, and the reason I wanted to create this resource. You have the power to change the world.

ABOUT THE AUTHORS

CEDRICK LAFLEUR MLS, (AMT)

Visionary Author of 3 books

Website: www.lafleurleadershipinstitute.com
E-Mail: cedrick@lafleurleadershipinstitute.com

Introducing Cedrick LaFleur, the epitome of a sales professional!

With an impressive track record spanning over 35+ years in the high-pressure world of medical device sales, Cedrick is a force to be reckoned with. He is the visionary author of ***The Blueprint for Manager Success***. In this anthology, Cedrick led seven other authors to write a leadership book designed to help aspiring managers develop the skills all frontline leaders need.

Million Dollar Beach House: My Journey to an EXTRAordinary Life. This book was personal, it is a true overcoming story. It describes his journey of getting married at 19, financial struggles, and the rebound. His rebound is an inspiring story of a poor, black kid from Lake Charles, La., developing goals, taking action steps to achieve those goals, building a successful corporate career, and letting nothing get in the way. In addition, you learn how he was able to retire at the age of 50 and build his dream beach house for cash. Get the book. Go to his website to check out the mini documentary. Be inspired to create your dream life.

Cedrick is a recently retired Regional Sales Leader at Abbott Laboratories after 22 years. Cedrick's expertise and leadership were instrumental in managing a staggering $1 billion dollar product line in Global Marketing. But that's not all! Cedrick also successfully ran a $33 million dollar sales region, stretching from Arizona to Tennessee.

Equipped with extensive training in various sales modalities, such as Face-to-Face, SPIN, and Consultative Sales, Cedrick is a true master in his field.

Cedrick celebrated 36 years of marriage to his wife, Tammie. This is a major accomplishment in his life, specifically because they got married at the young ages of 19 and 17, respectively.

Cedrick is an Abbott Chairman's Award winner for leading Abbott's response to Hurricane Katrina for La, MS, AL, and Texas. This award is the highest honor that an Abbott employee can earn.

Cedrick is the Chief Executive at LaFleur Leadership Institute, which focuses on building **the best-in-class** leaders. He has built LaFleur Leadership Institute into a multi-six-figure business model.

Cedrick is the proud father of two children, TreKessa (TK, 36) and Patrick (31), and recently became a proud grandfather to Jose Carlos (JC).

TYWAUNA WILSON, MBA, MLS(ASCP)^{CM}

Award-Winning Laboratory Leader, International Trainer, and Coach

Website: www.trendyelitellc.com
E-Mail: info@trendyelitellc.com

Tywauna Wilson, MBA, MLS(ASCP)^{CM} is a leader in the medical laboratory industry, a sought-after speaker, coach, mentor, and author of the book "Some Leaders Wear Lab Coats". She is the complete package when it comes to helping new and emerging leaders reach their goals with career advancement. With 20 years of progressive healthcare and laboratory leadership experience, Tywauna has trained leaders around the world on leadership and career strategies, including in Rwanda, Africa. She is a graduate of Kentucky State and Indiana Wesleyan universities, where she received her Bachelor of Science in Clinical Laboratory Science and MBA, respectively.

Tywauna Wilson, Mba, Mls(ascp)cm

With several accolades, including the 2023 ASCP Mentor Award, 2023 Diversity MBA Top 100 Under 50 Emerging Leader Award, 2021 ASCP Career Ambassador Award, 2021 Cardinal Health Laboratory Excellence List Advocacy Winner, and 2017 ASCP Forty Under 40, Tywauna is more than qualified to show professionals how to unleash their star power, grow, succeed, and transform their careers.

As the President of Trendy Elite Coaching and Consulting, Tywauna has developed best-in-class leaders through her Standout Leader Academy, leadership training, coaching, and mentoring programs. She also hosts two popular podcasts, "eLABorate Topics" and "Leadership Tidbits® with Coach Tee Wilson," which are full of inspiring advice, invaluable tips, and actionable strategies for career success.

For Professionals focused on career advancement, Tywauna is the perfect mentor. Through her book, "Some Leaders Wear Lab Coats" or her leadership series, "Leadership Tidbits," she gives practical tips to go beyond your competence and increase your credibility, visibility, and influence to become a sought-after leader in your industry. Her mission is "to empower and train one million leaders to be able to lead with confidence and have careers that make them proud."

www.ingramcontent.com/pod-product-compliance
Lightning Source LLC
Chambersburg PA
CBHW050112170426
43198CB00014B/2544